RATINGS

Excellent	4 points
Good	3 points
Average	2 points
Acceptable	1 point

TECHNIQUE CUE AND RATING SHEET

		Rating periods											
		1	2	3	4	5	6	7	8	9	10	11	12
Position at keyboard	**Rating**												
1. Sits in a comfortable, relaxed position directly in front of keyboard.													
2. Keeps feet on floor for proper body balance.													
3. Keeps elbows in relaxed, natural position at sides of body.													
Keystroking	**Rating**												
1. Keeps fingers curved and upright over home keys.													
2. Strikes each key with proper finger.													
3. Keeps hands and arms quiet, wrists low.													
4. Makes quick, snappy keystrokes with immediate key release.													
Space bar	**Rating**												
1. Keeps right thumb curved and close to space bar.													
2. Strikes space bar with a quick, down-and-in (toward palm) motion of thumb.													
3. Releases space bar instantly.													
4. Does not pause before or after spacing stroke.													
Return key	**Rating**												
1. Returns quickly at ends of lines.													
2. Strikes return key with right little finger; then, fingers on home keys.													
3. Keeps eyes on source copy during and following return.													
4. Starts new line without a pause.													
Shift keys	**Rating**												
1. Reaches quickly with little fingers; keeps other fingers on home row.													
2. Depresses shift key as the character key is struck.													
3. Releases shift key quickly after character is struck.													
4. Does not pause before or after shift-key stroke.													
Tabulator	**Rating**												
1. Reaches quickly with left little finger.													
2. Keeps other fingers near home keys.													
3. Keeps eyes on source copy as tabulator is used.													
4. Continues keying after tabulating--without pauses.													
	Total												

RATINGS	
Excellent	4 points
Good	3 points
Average	2 points
Acceptable	1 point

TECHNIQUE CUE AND RATING SHEET, continued

		Rating periods											
		1	2	3	4	5	6	7	8	9	10	11	12
Reading/ keying response patterns	**Rating**												
1. Keeps eyes on source copy; concentrates on copy to be keyed													
2. Maintains continuous keystroking by reading slightly ahead in the copy; keys fluently.													
3. Keys balanced-hand words by *word* response.													
4. Keys one-hand words by *letter* response.													
5. Blends *word* and *letter* responses into a smooth, fluent rhythm pattern that varies according to difficulty of copy.													
Mind-set	**Rating**												
1. Follows directions carefully.													
2. Gives attention to technique cues.													
3. Makes effort to reach suggested goals.													
4. Practices with a purpose.													
5. Appears alert, but shows no evidence of undue tension in shoulders, arms, and hands.													
	Total												

Rating Plan

1. Your instructor may observe and rate you on each technique category listed on this Rating Sheet (or those that are currently appropriate), using point scores of 4 = A; 3 = B; 2 = C; 1= D. The appropriate point score may be entered opposite the word *Rating* for each technique being rated.
2. A checkmark opposite a numbered item indicates a need for immediate improvement.
3. Add (down) the *Rating* scores awarded for each technique and enter the total in the *Total* cell.
4. Divide the total by the number of techniques rated.
5. Determine your technique grade from the scale at the right.

Average Rating		Grade
3.6 - 4.0	=	A
2.6 - 3.5	=	B
1.6 - 2.5	=	C
0.6 - 1.5	=	D
0 - 0.5	=	F

Basic skill improvement record--speed

use in Division 1

The charts given here may be used to record *gwam* on 1', 2', and 3'**straight-copy** timed writings.

To plot *gwam* on each writing to be recorded, place a dot on the vertical line at the point opposite the proper number (*gwam*).

To show your progress, connect the dots with a solid line.

Note: Your *gwam* will increase gradually, with the right kind of practice. You likely will progress faster at first than you will later.

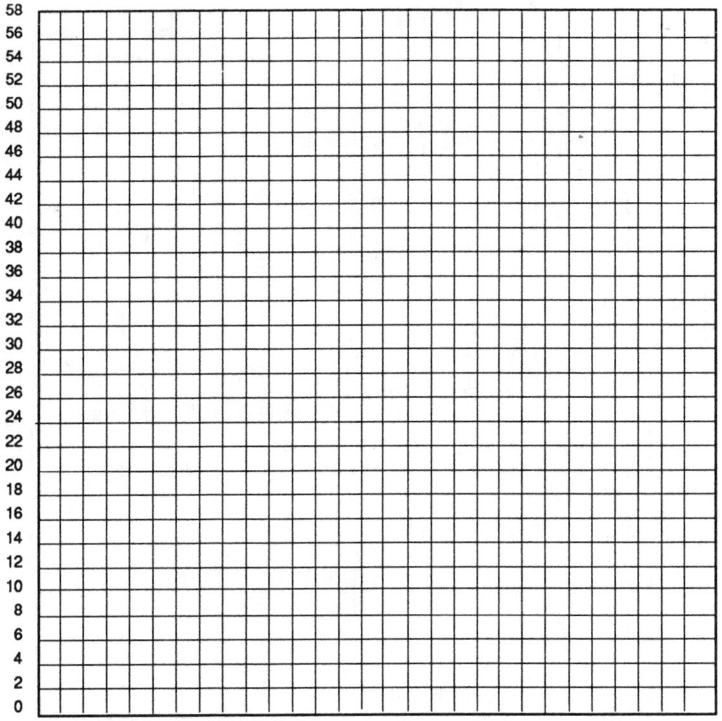

1' straight-copy sentences

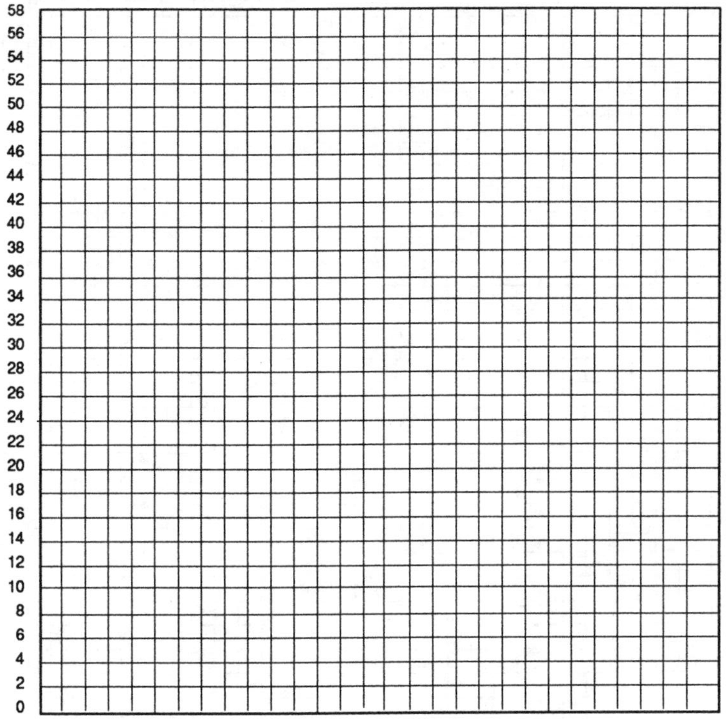

1' straight-copy paragraphs

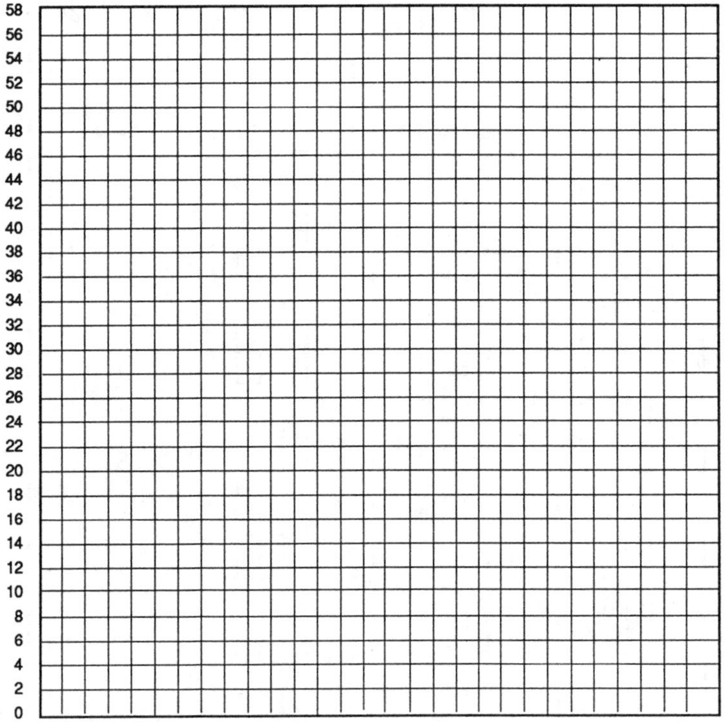

2' straight-copy paragraphs

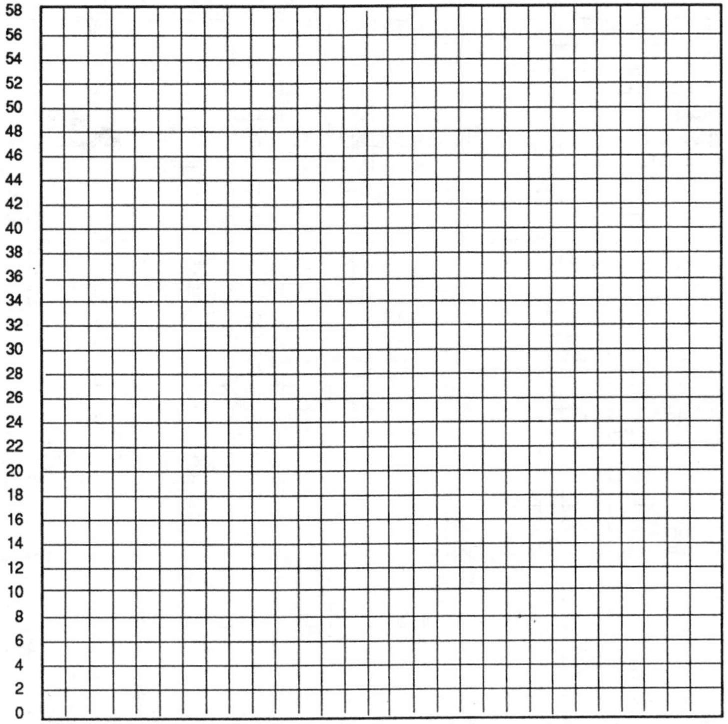

3' straight copy paragraphs

Basic skill improvement record--speed

use in Division 1

The charts given here may be used to record *gwam* on 5' timed writings on **straight copy** and 3' writings on **script, rough-draft,** and **statistical** copy.

To plot *gwam* on each writing to be recorded, place a dot on the vertical line at the point opposite the proper number (*gwam*).

To show your progress, connect the dots with a solid line.

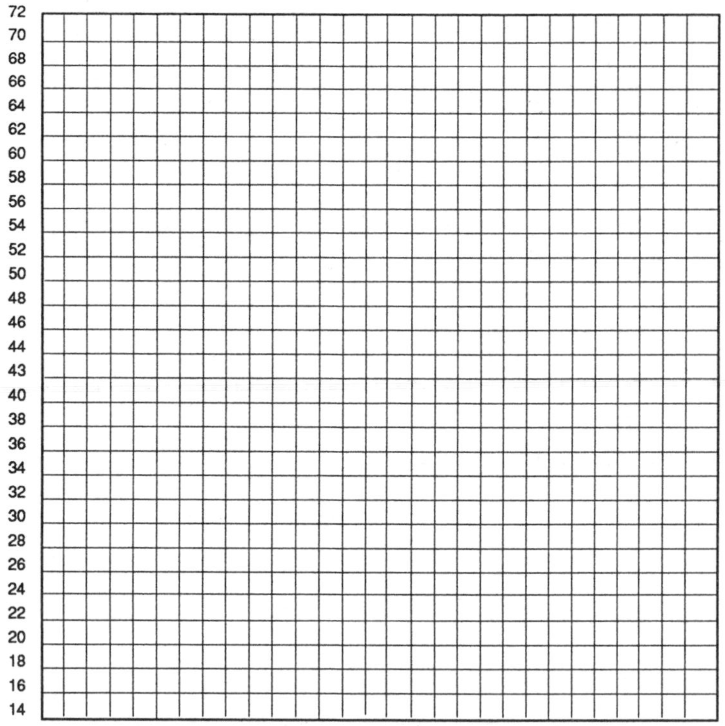

5' straight-copy paragraphs

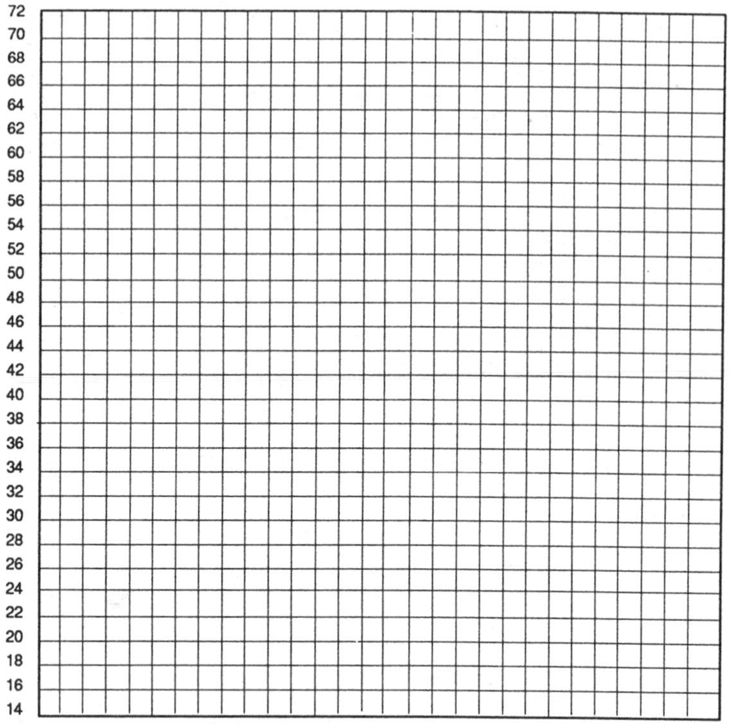

3' statistical-copy paragraphs

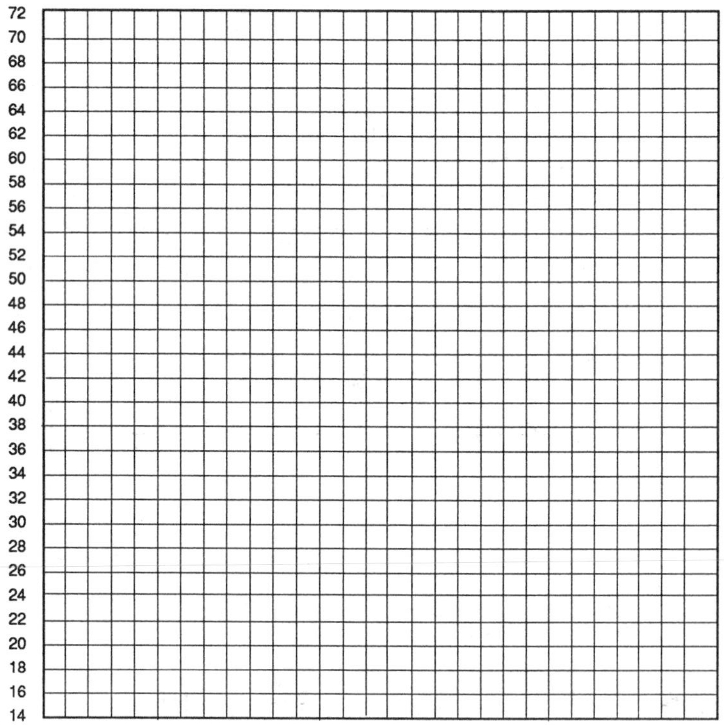

3' script-copy paragraphs

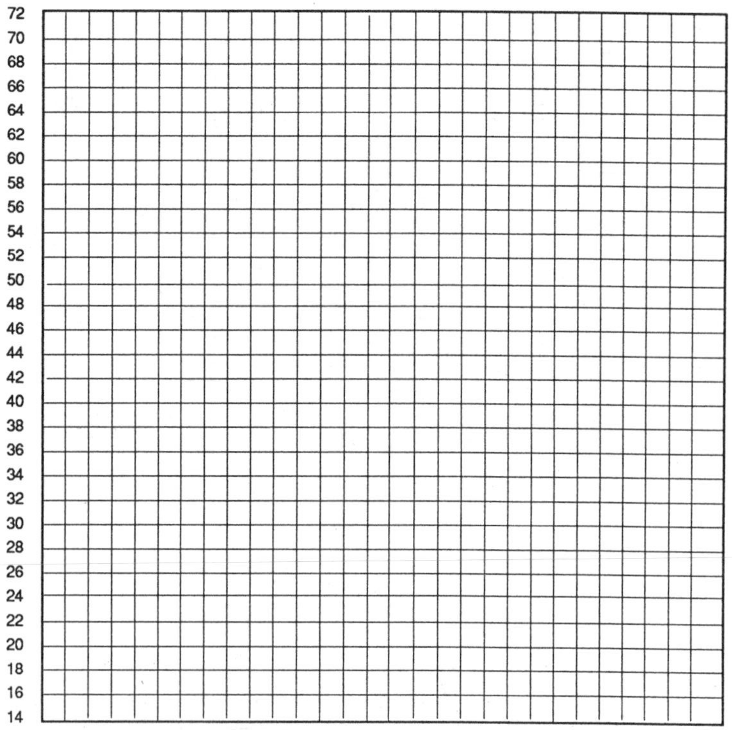

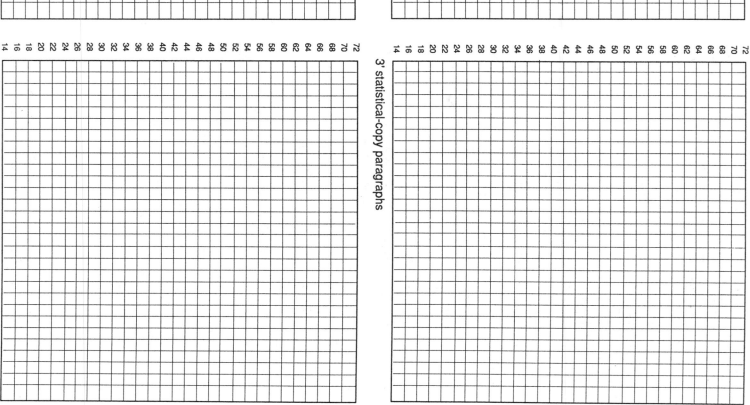

3' rough-draft paragraphs

Basic skill improvement record--accuracy

use in Division 1

The charts given here may be used to record the number of *errors* on 1', 2', and 3' straight-copy timed writings.

To plot *errors* on each writing to be recorded, place a dot on the vertical line at the point opposite the proper number (*errors*).

To show your progress, connect the dots with a solid line.

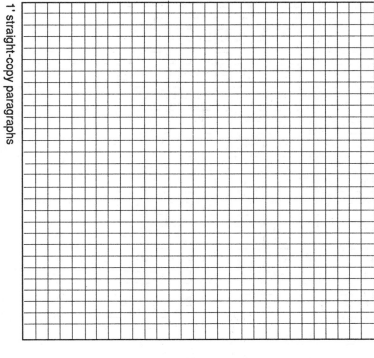

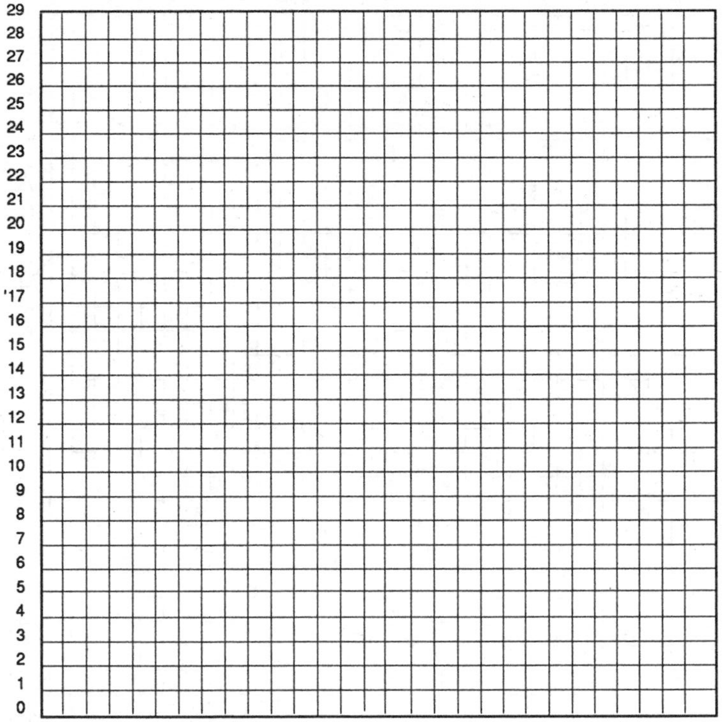

1' straight-copy paragraphs

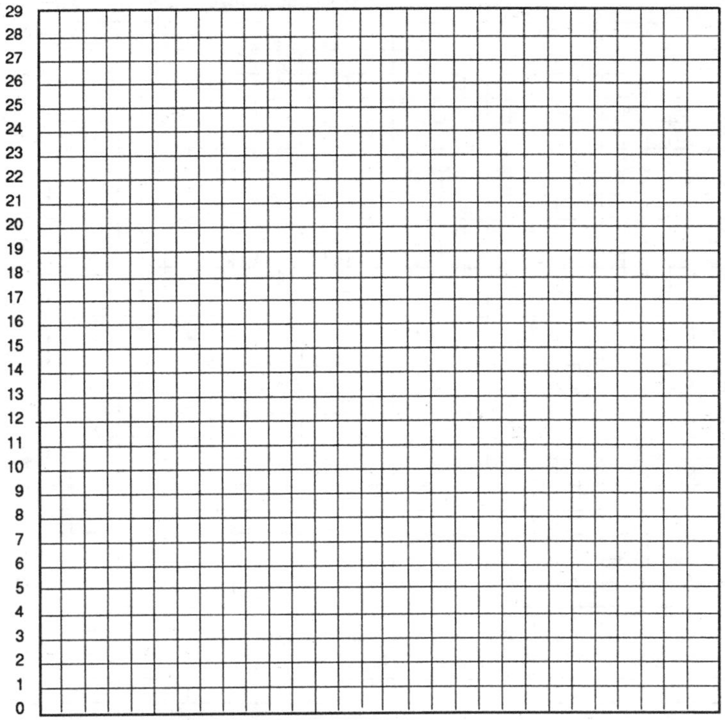

1' straight-copy paragraphs

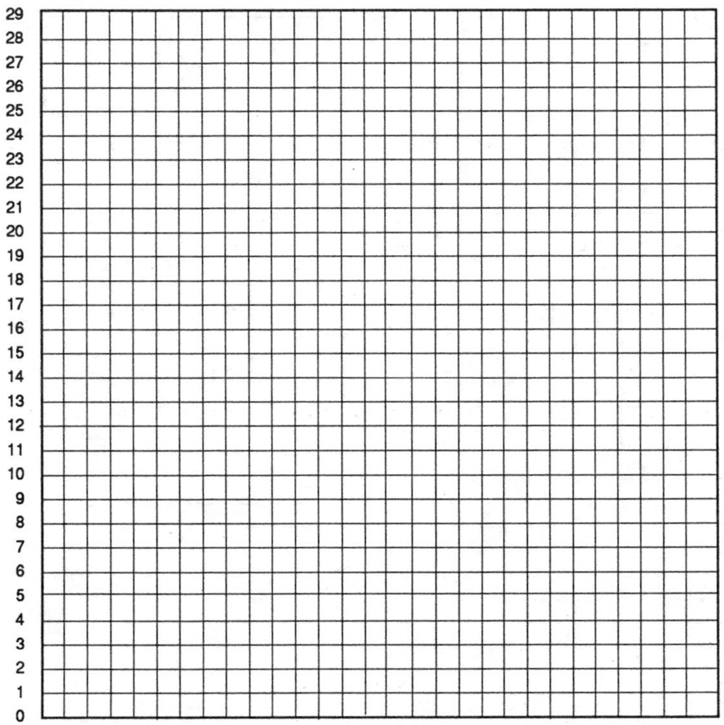

2' straight-copy paragraphs

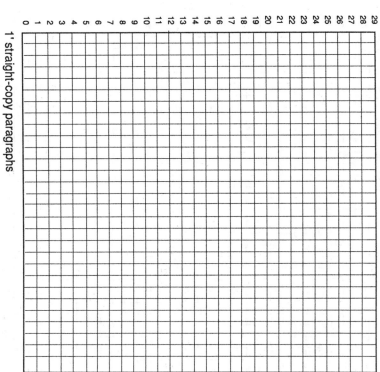

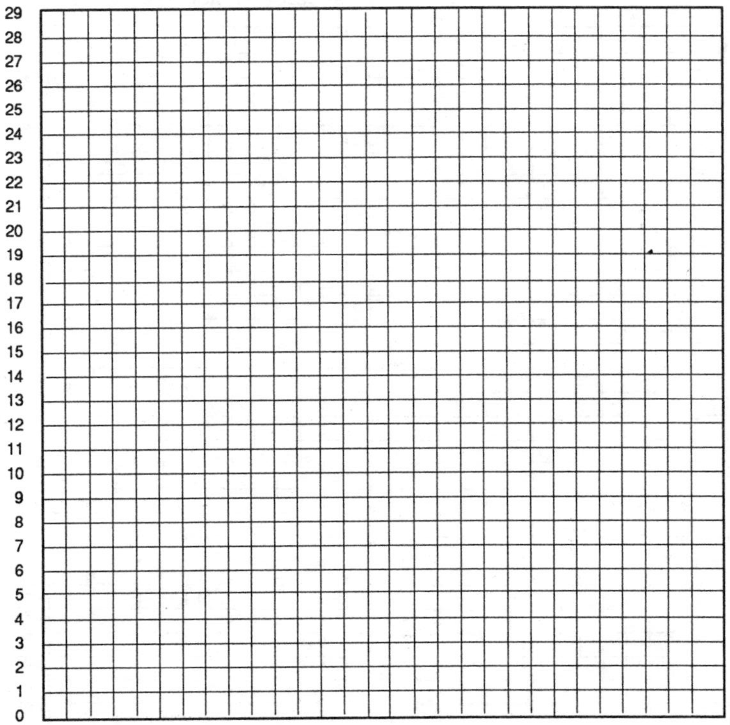

3' straight-copy paragraphs

Basic skill improvement record--accuracy

use in Division 1

The charts given here may be used to record the number of *errors* on 5' timed writings on **straight copy** and 3' timed writings on **script, rough-draft,** and **statistical copy**.

To plot *errors* on each writing to be recorded, place a dot on the vertical line at the point opposite the proper number (*errors*).

To show your progress, connect the dots with a solid line.

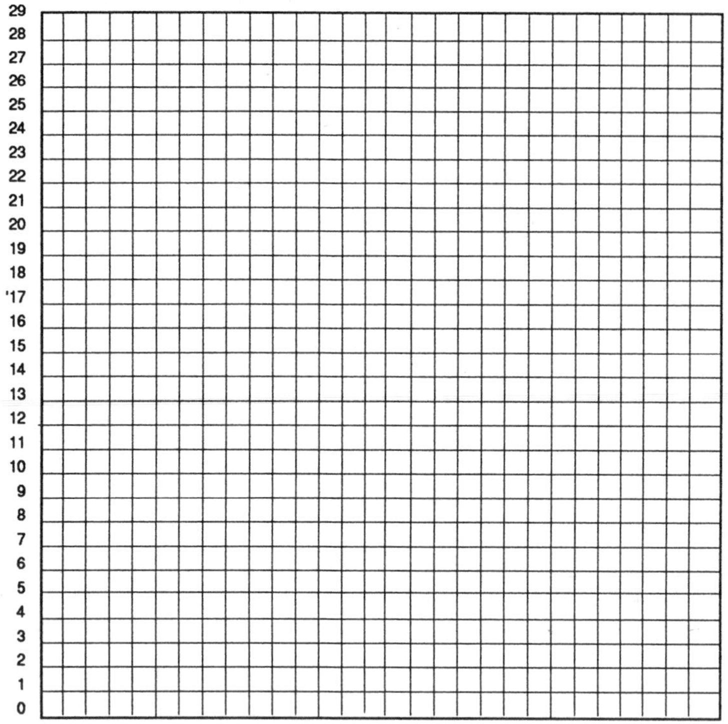

5' straight-copy paragraphs

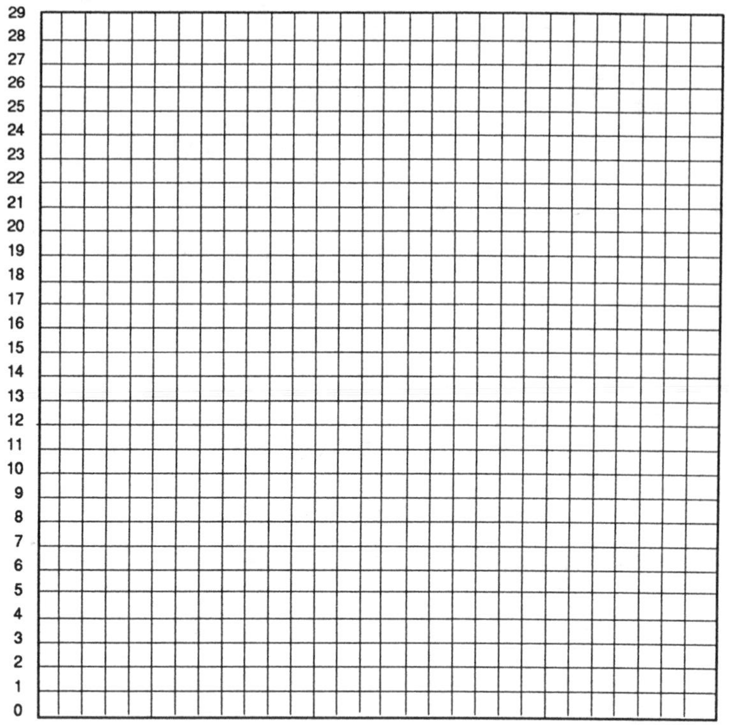

3' statistical-copy paragraphs

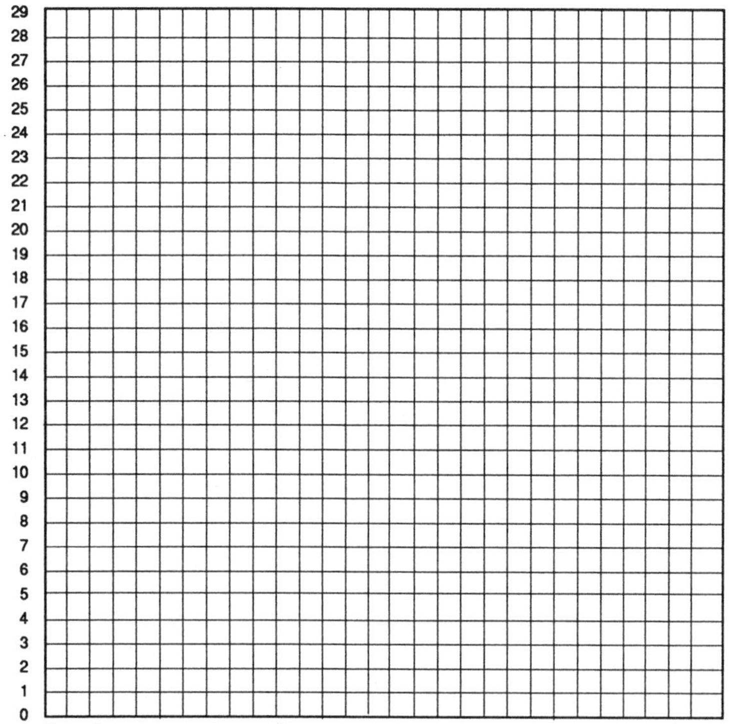

3' script-copy paragraphs

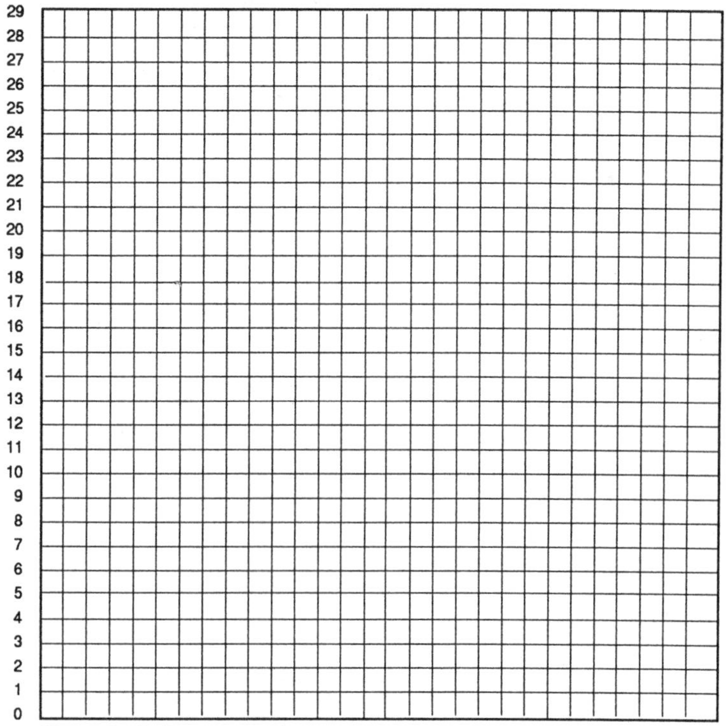

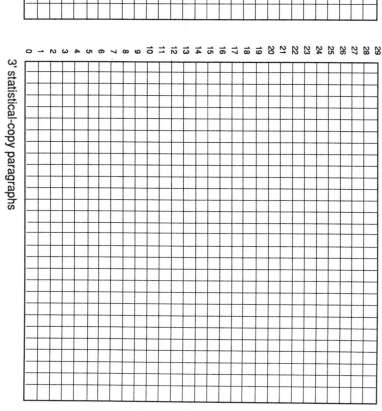

3' rough-draft paragraphs

PROGRESS RECORD FOR DIVISION 1

PROCEDURE Keep a lesson-by-lesson completion record on the form given below, indicating your speed and accuracy on timed writings and the number of problems completed.

LESSON	DATE	GWAM (Gross Words a Minute)/ERRORS				NUMBER OF PROBLEMS COMPLETED
		1' Timing	3' Timing	5' Timing	Other Timing	
13						
14						
15						
16						
17						
18						
19						
20						
21						
22						
23						
24						
25						
26						
27						
28						
29						
30						
31						
32						
33						
34						
35						
36						
37						
38						
39						
40						
41						
42						
43						
44						
45						
46						
47						
48						
49						
50						

Learn to use end-of-line columns and scales

The first column at the right of each sentence shows the number of 5-stroke words it contains. The second column shows *gwam* if the sentence is completed in 30". If the sentence is not completed, use the below-the-last-line scale (multiply that number by 2 for a 30" writing). Thus, if you take a 1' writing on the sentences at the right and key through the word *proficient* in Sentence 3, you will have reached 19 *gwam*. If you take a 30" writing on Sentence 4 and key through *bit*, you will have reached 14 *gwam*.

Complete Items 1-3; then check correct answers at the bottom of the page.

		words	*gwam* 30"
1	Blair kept fuel for the autos.	6	12
2	The goal is to rid the lake of rot.	7	14
3	Rowland Burns is proficient but haughty.	8	16
4	Did he laugh when the turkey bit the corncob?	9	18
5	Did the men own the shanty by the end of the lane?	10	20

gwam 1' | 1 | 2 | 3 | 4 | 5 | 6 | 7 | 8 | 9 | 10 |

Answers

1. If you take a 1' writing on the sentences above and key through the word *Did* in the fourth sentence, your *gwam* will be (a) 22; (b) 30; (c) 34 .... ______
2. If, when taking a 30" writing on the fourth sentence, you complete the sentence, your *gwam* will be (a) 9; (b) 15; (c) 18 .... ______
3. If, when taking a 30" writing on the fifth sentence, you key through *end*, your *gwam* will be (a) 9; (b) 16; (c) 19 .... ______

Learn to use superior figures, word-count columns, and scales with paragraphs

The superior dots and figures in each paragraph indicate the number of words keyed during a 1' writing of each paragraph (the count increases in 2-word increments). The columns at the right of the paragraphs show the cumulative line-by-line gross words keyed during a 2' writing on both paragraphs. The 2' *gwam* scale below the last line shows the number of words keyed for a partial line during a 2' writing. Thus, if you take a 1' writing on the first paragraph and key through the word *in* in the second line, you will have reached 16 *gwam*. If you take a 2' writing on both ¶s and key through the word *our* in the second line of the second ¶, you will have reached 21 *gwam*. Complete items 4-6; then check correct answers.

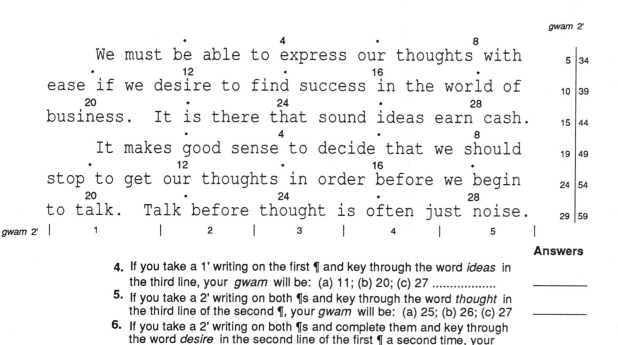

	gwam 2'	
• 4 • 8 We must be able to express our thoughts with	5	34
• 12 • 16 • ease if we desire to find success in the world of	10	39
20 • 24 • 28 business. It is there that sound ideas earn cash.	15	44
• 4 • 8 It makes good sense to decide that we should	19	49
• 12 • 16 • stop to get our thoughts in order before we begin	24	54
20 • 24 • 28 to talk. Talk before thought is often just noise.	29	59

gwam 2' | 1 | 2 | 3 | 4 | 5 |

Answers

4. If you take a 1' writing on the first ¶ and key through the word *ideas* in the third line, your *gwam* will be: (a) 11; (b) 20; (c) 27 .... ______
5. If you take a 2' writing on both ¶s and key through the word *thought* in the third line of the second ¶, your *gwam* will be: (a) 25; (b) 26; (c) 27 ______
6. If you take a 2' writing on both ¶s and complete them and key through the word *desire* in the second line of the first ¶ a second time, your *gwam* will be: (a) 36; (b) 31; (c) 34 .... ______

Answers: 1. a; 2. c; 3. b; 4. c; 5. c; 6. a

Basic skill: alphabet review

for use after Lesson 12

Key each line twice (slowly, then faster); rekey lines that seem difficult.

Keep fingers curved and upright over home row; reach with fingers, keeping hands still.

Note: Each sentence (*a-z*) contains at least 4 uses of the letter emphasized. Each *alphabet* sentence contains all letters of the alphabet.

a	Eating an apple quickly gave Aaron a stomach ache.
b	Bob and Billy drove to the beach because Barb did.
c	Caramel candy can cause Carl to become sick today.
d	Danny watched Dad's dog destroy Dug's sand castle.
e	The rewards were presented after the banquet meal.
f	Francine favored flavorful fresh fruits for lunch.
g	Georgia forgot to get ghosts and goblins for Gary.
h	Henry had heard that Hank had hit a handsome hero.
i	Inquiries regarding university tuition are mailed.
j	The judge and jury jointly made the just judgment.
k	A kind bookkeeper drank a soda and joked with Kim.
l	Lovely Lisa likes the luscious and silky lipstick.
m	Many masked mummers performed in merry pantomimes.
n	A personnel manager cannot know a company nominee.
o	Only one location on the ocean is good for profit.
p	Philip properly prepared the police proposal plan.
q	It was quite late when they quietly quit quilting.
r	Roger and Kerri may drive a red car to their prom.
s	Professor Steven Simpson teaches business classes.
t	Attempt to get total control as you key for speed.
u	Undue or unjust pressure can usurp your authority.
v	Every villian will evade very vigorous vigilantes.
w	The town will wage war on sewage and wasted water.
x	An extremely excited Max is excused from the exam.
y	A young Yorkshire puppy is eating my berry yogurt.
z	Dizzy Zelda went to the zoo to see the zany zebra.
alphabet	Bo Vend saw quick hares jog past a lazy swamp fox.
alphabet	Levi Zwicker acquired Bix's jalopy for prom night.
alphabet	Did Jet Wazel quickly bring phlox for Mick's vase?
alphabet	I just paid Boz for very quickly writing the exam.

| 1 | 2 | 3 | 4 | 5 | 6 | 7 | 8 | 9 | 10 |

Basic skill: keystroking precision

for use after Lesson 12

Key lines 1 and 2 of each group 3 times; then key line 3 of each group; check for substitution errors.

Keep hands and arms still as you reach *up* to third row and *down* to first row.

Note: Each group of lines emphasizes common letter substitutions. These are listed in order of frequency of occurrence.

t	at fat hat sat to tip the that they fast last slat
r	or red try ran run air era fair rid ride trip trap
t/r	A trainer sprained an arm trying to tame the bear.
m	am me my mine jam man more most dome month minimum
n	no an now nine once net knee name ninth know never
m/n	Many men and women are important company managers.
o	on or to not now one oil toil over only solo today
i	it is in tie did fix his sit like with insist will
o/i	Joni will consider obtaining options to buy coins.
a	at an as art has and any case data haze tart smart
s	us as so say sat slap lass class just sassy simple
a/s	Disaster was averted as the steamer sailed to sea.
e	we he ear the key her hear chef desire where there
i	it in fit fail wise coil knit this itemize utility
e/i	An expression of gratitude for service is desired.
s	is his see sea list bass mast last rust must games
d	do did add bad day sad send debt card doses sudden
s/d	The sea's sudden misdeed destroyed goods or lands.
r	or for row rag ever near for rare wrote their area
e	we sea eat here seem year real earn eager receiver
r/e	I heard a remark regarding her recent termination.
v	via vow van dive over live vice above brave divide
b	be by but buy bat been bank back about body before
v/b	Everybody voted to give a beverage to a brave boy.
w	we way was why few were went when work while water
e	err the key ease deny time even eager where weekly
w/e	Working women wear sweaters when weather dictates.
e	he we she her elf end deal deaf exits erode eleven
d	do dip bid bed debt dude delay dress decide differ
e/d	Edie decided to deduct expenses for making a deed.

| 1 | 2 | 3 | 4 | 5 | 6 | 7 | 8 | 9 | 10 |

Basic skill: goal sentences

for use after Lesson 12

Key both lines of a 2-line group as a 1' writing. Listen for the 30" guide; try to reach the end of each line as "return" is called.

Note: Line 1 of each group contains easy balanced-hand words; Line 2, more difficult words.

		words	30"
1	He held the big dog.	4	8
2	We can only see Jon.	4	8
1	By the chapel is the oak.	5	10
2	Few awards are presented.	5	10
1	The busy guru is the rye heir.	6	12
2	Drew gazed at a hilly raceway.	6	12
1	Envy is an element of dormant fury.	7	14
2	Tea will be served at that regatta.	7	14
1	The ivory gown is an eighth enchantment.	8	16
2	A million readers link cause and effect.	8	16
1	The haughty maid is to end the fight with me.	9	18
2	Gaze at stars, stare at seas, and stay brave.	9	18
1	He is to blame for all their right field problems.	10	20
2	Many were vexed because wages were severely taxed.	10	20

| 1 | 2 | 3 | 4 | 5 | 6 | 7 | 8 | 9 | 10 |

1 Key a 1' writing on each sentence in the Goal Set; determine *average gwam;* add 2 words (*goal gwam*). Find your *goal gwam* (approx.) in either the 30" or 20" column (Progressive set), as indicated by your instructor.
2 Key a 1' guided writing on the sentence matching your *goal gwam*; try to reach the end of the sentence as "return" is called.
3 If you meet your goal, continue to the next sentence.
4 Repeat Steps 2 and 3, attempting to reach your maximum speed.

Note: The sentences are loaded with easy balanced-hand words to promote speed.

		words	30"	20"
	Goal set:			
1	An endowment did entitle them to go to the island.	10		
2	Jane is to go to town by autobus, but she is busy.	10		
	Progressive set:			
1	Lay down the jai alai memento.	6	12	18
2	The antique bicycle is by the dorm.	7	14	21
3	Sue may spend the usual for six turkeys.	8	16	24
4	Bob did fight for the handiwork of the corps.	9	18	27
5	A handy man did mend their socks and fix the auto.	10	20	30

| 1 | 2 | 3 | 4 | 5 | 6 | 7 | 8 | 9 | 10 |

Self-check questions 1

for use after Lesson 12

NAME ____________________

DATE ____________ SCORE ________

1 Write the letter for each correct answer in the blank at the right.

2 When you have answered all the items, check your answers below. (The answer appears on the textbook page shown in parentheses.)

Answers	Text Page
1. b	9
2. c	1
3. b	4
4. a	4
5. a	4

Answers	Text Page
6. b	4
7. a	16
8. c	16
9. b	16
10. a	17

Answers	Text Page
11. a	20
12. c	25
13. a	25
14. c	27
15. b	27

Answers	Text Page
16. a	27
17. b	28
18. c	29
19. c	29
20. c	29

answers score

1. When operating a keyboard, wrists should be (a) touching the frame, (b) low but not touching the frame, or (c) arched. .... ____ 1. ____
2. The paper guide is used to (a) remove a sheet of paper, (b) support the paper after it is in place, or (c) guide the left edge of the paper as it is being inserted. .... ____ 2. ____
3. To leave one blank line, strike the return key (a) one time, (b) two times, or (c) three times. .... ____ 3. ____
4. A double space contains (a) one blank line, (b) two blank lines, or (c) four blank lines. .... ____ 4. ____
5. Pica type is (a) 10 pitch, (b) 12 pitch, or (c) 15 pitch. .... ____ 5. ____
6. Elite type is (a) larger than pica, (b) smaller than pica, or (c) the same size as pica. .... ____ 6. ____
7. After a period following an initial or an abbreviation, (a) space one time, (b) space two times, or (c) do not space. .... ____ 7. ____
8. After a period at the end of a line, (a) space one time, (b) space two times, or (c) do not space. .... ____ 8. ____
9. After a period used as ending punctuation within a line, space (a) one time, (b) two times, or (c) three times. .... ____ 9. ____
10. After a semicolon within a line, (a) space one time, (b) space two times, or (c) do not space. .... ____ 10. ____
11. GWAM is (a) total words keyed, (b) total words keyed correctly, or (c) total words containing errors. .... ____ 11. ____
12. After a comma at the end of a line, (a) space one time, (b) space two times, or (c) do not space. .... ____ 12. ____
13. After a comma within a line, (a) space one time, (b) space two times, or (c) do not space. .... ____ 13. ____
14. After a beginning quotation mark, (a) space one time, (b) space two times, or (c) do not space. .... ____ 14. ____
15. HFW is (a) the number of difficult words, (b) the number of frequently used words, or (c) the number of commonly misspelled words. ...... ____ 15. ____
16. SI is (a) the number of syllables per word, (b) the number of syllables per line, or (c) the number of syllables per paragraph. .... ____ 16. ____
17. When a colon is used to introduce a statement within a line, space (a) one time and begin the statement with a capital letter, (b) two times and begin the statement with a capital letter, (c) two times and begin the statement with a lower-case letter. .... ____ 17. ____
18. After a colon used to indicate time, (a) space one time, (b) space two times, or (c) do not space. .... ____ 18. ____
19. An apostrophe shows (a) omission of letters, (b) possession, or (c) both a and b. .... ____ 19. ____
20. After an apostrophe, (a) space one time, (b) space two times, or (c) do not space. .... ____ 20. ____

Page line gauge

Place this line gauge behind a plain sheet with the numbers extending beyond the right edge of the paper.

Use the numbers for positioning report page numbers, headings, etc.

1" SIDE MARGIN OR 6 1/2" LINE

1" FROM EDGES

1 1/2" SIDE MARGIN

1 1/2" FROM EDGES

2" SIDE MARGIN

2" FROM EDGES

4" LINE

2" FROM EDGES

5" LINE

1 1/2" FROM EDGES

6" LINE

1" FROM EDGES

Formatting applications 1

for use after Lesson 15

a
Tabulator

begin on line 10

1 Set a 60-space line.
2 Clear all present tab stops.
3 Set tabs 18, 36, and 54 spaces from the left margin; return.
4 Key the first word; tab; key the second word; continue to end of line; return.
5 Repeat Steps 1-4 for the rest of the lines.

	12+18	12+36	12+54
1 during	office	please	policy
2 amount	review	return	either
3 reason	recent	advise	annual
4 cannot	fiscal	family	access
5 budget	toward	health	estate

b
Line lengths

begin 2" from top of page

1 Set a 50-space line. (Do not use automatic return, though the feature may be available.) Set a tab for a 5-space ¶ indention.
2 Reset the line ending (right margin) 5 spaces to the right.
3 Key both ¶s; listen for the line end signal as you key. When you hear the signal, complete the word you are keying, using the typewriter margin release if needed. Return and continue the remaining lines.
4 Set a 60-space line; then reset the line ending 5 spaces to the right. Repeat Step 2.
5 Set a 70-space line; then reset the line ending 5 spaces to the right. Repeat Step 2.

Note: Your keyed line endings will not match those below.

Sometimes college life can be rather uneventful and boring. When this happens, some students consider dropping out of college to work in the "real world." This decision can be regretted later in life.

College students who get involved in extracurricular activities are seldom bored. For these individuals, college provides a chance to develop leadership abilities and to enjoy an active social life.

c
Announcement

Format the announcement on a full sheet. Center the announcement vertically; center each line horizontally.

Delta Delta Delta Sorority's
ANNUAL "SHOOT THE HOOCH"
Open Social
All spring, summer, and fall rushees
are invited to attend this event
on the Chattahoochee River

Basic skill: figure review

for use after Lesson 20

Key each line twice (slowly, then faster); rekey lines that seem difficult.

Keep fingers curved and upright over home row; reach with fingers, keeping hands still.

Figures

1 Export 38 cans on May 17; 50 cans on May 26; retain 49 cans.
2 Did 15 girls visit the museum at 4983 Orient or 3670 Laguna?
3 On May 10, 26 of us took Vans 39 and 47 the 58 miles to Rio.
4 He has 67 cows, 39 pigs, 14 ducks, 280 chickens, and 5 cats.
5 Send Lew 38 No. 50 panes and 26 No. 49 sheets on October 17.
6 I planted 1,586 acres of corn, 493 of wheat, and 270 of rye.
7 Cy will be 19 on May 30; Jan, 48 on May 27; Dee, 56 in July.
8 Question 59: If 24 of 87 boys go on May 10, will 63 remain?
9 A group of 105 men and 98 women left on Route 376 on May 24.
10 I live at 46 East 93d; Ky, at 28 Lynn; Bob, at 17 West 50th.

| 1 | 2 | 3 | 4 | 5 | 6 | 7 | 8 | 9 | 10 | 11 | 12 |

Basic skill: symbol review

for use after Lesson 25

Key each line twice (slowly, then faster); rekey lines that seem difficult.

Symbols

1 Hey! Joe! Stop the bus! There's the gate! We're on time!
2 Only first-class papers have these up-to-the minute reviews.
3 Can't Nan's sister read Luis' poem? It's Luis' finest work.
4 Bayton (her team) and Owens (his team) play tonight (Friday).
5 "I'm eager," I stated, "to create a trade union in my area."
6 S & A has orders from Kena & Forle, T & T, and Kalt & Paley.
7 Did Rita and/or Chen walk/run in the relays? Did she/he go?
8 To: Joe Abt From: Lou Posa Subject: Our trip to Peoria.
9 Maria--she's my sister--and Bob--my brother--skate together.
10 Hey! Isn't our first-bell class (accounting) in A & M Hall?

| 1 | 2 | 3 | 4 | 5 | 6 | 7 | 8 | 9 | 10 | 11 | 12 |

Basic skill: figure/symbol review

for use after Lesson 25

Key each line twice (slowly, then faster); rekey lines that seem difficult.

Figures and Symbols

1 I use 15% for food; 35%, lodging; 5%, clothing; 5%, savings.
2 The price was $47; I paid $45 and saved $49. Jan saved $44.
3 The #3 dies are $4, the #2 dies are $3, the #1 dies are $12.
4 Is 2/3 more than 1/3? Does she know? Is 5/8 more than 2/4?
5 Of my cases (90) for 7 & 7 Taxis, I won 79 and lost only 11!
6 I need $86: $9 for cab, $35 for dinner, and $42 for a show.
7 My tattered--85% nylon--$45 sweater deserved no better care.
8 Order 3# of #8 rye, $6; 5# of #10, $9; and 4# of #2 rye, $7.
9 I set $345 (up 15%) as a link-up fee in my West Ohio TV area.
10 On 9/7, I set my #45 reverse gear in a pull-open cedar case.

| 1 | 2 | 3 | 4 | 5 | 6 | 7 | 8 | 9 | 10 | 11 | 12 |

Basic skill: measurement

for use after Lesson 25

a
Straight copy

1 Set margins for a 60-space line.
2 Key two 1' writings on each ¶; determine *gwam ;* proofread and circle any errors.
3 Key two 3' writings on both ¶s combined; determine *gwam* ; proofread and circle any errors.

all letters used **E 1.2 si 5.1 awl 90% hfw** *gwam* 3'

A dealer in stocks and bonds is called a broker. Most 4
stocks are sold in stock exchanges. The price at which a per- 8
son can buy or sell a stock is publicized in a stock report 12
or journal each day. When people wish to buy or sell a stock, 16
they call their dealers. 18

People often wish to put some of their earnings in stocks 22
of their choice. They go to a stock dealer and order a quan- 26
tity of stocks they wish to buy. A very small fee is charged 30
for this help. This charge is paid along with the cost of the 34
stock. 35

gwam 3' | 1 | 2 | 3 | 4 |

b
Statistical copy

1 Set margins for a 60-space line.
2 Key two 1' writings on each ¶; determine *gwam ;* proofread and circle any errors.
3 Key two 3' writings on both ¶s combined; determine *gwam* ; proofread and circle any errors.

all letters/figures used **E 1.2 si 5.1 awl 90% hfw** *gwam* 3'

A quiz on Chapter 6 of your text will be given today. 4
Just bring with you a #2 pencil and $1 (to pay for the use of 8
the test materials). 9

A 10% bonus will be offered--but it is for a very hard- 13
to-answer question! A review will be given at 4:25 today. 17

Do read Chapters 7 and 8 and the article "It's the Law 21
of the Land" for 10/3; bring with you $9 if you plan to take 25
the field trip. 26

gwam 3' | 1 | 2 | 3 | 4 |

Self-check questions 2

for use after Lesson 31

NAME ____________________

DATE ____________ SCORE __________

1 Write the letter for each correct answer in the blank at the right.

2 When you have answered all the items, check your answers below.

Answers	Text Page
1. a	37
2. c	37
3. b	37
4. c	37
5. c	39

Answers	Text Page
6. a	40
7. a	40
8. c	41
9. b	41
10. b	41

Answers	Text Page
11. a	42
12. a	50
13. b	54
14. b	54
15. c	69

Answers	Text Page
16. a	69
17. c	69
18. b	74
19. b	69
20. a	73

	answers	score
1. The center point of a writing line when 10-pitch (pica) type is used is (a) 42, (b) 51, or (c) 63.	____	1. ____
2. When using 12-pitch, a line in a standard 8 1/2" x 11" sheet of paper will accommodate (a) 85 characters, (b) 102 characters, or (c) 127 characters.	____	2. ____
3. Margins for an exact 60-space line using 10-pitch type are (a) 15 and 75, (b) 12 and 72, or (c) 10 and 70.	____	3. ____
4. Proportional spacing will accommodate (a) 10 spaces per inch, (b) 12 spaces per inch, or (c) a variable number of spaces per inch.	____	4. ____
5. Automatic return/word wrap will (a) automatically align copy at the right margin, (b) automatically hyphenate a word at the end of a line if necessary, or (c) automatically begin a new line at the left margin.	____	5. ____
6. To center a line (without automatic center feature), tab to the center point and (a) backspace one for each two characters, (b) backspace one for each character, or (c) begin keying the line.	____	6. ____
7. When backspacing to center a line, treat a "leftover" character as follows: (a) drop the character, (b) backspace one for the character, or (c) carry the character to the next line.	____	7. ____
8. A standard size sheet of paper contains (a) 54 lines, (b) 60 lines, or (c) 66 lines.	____	8. ____
9. When centering 10 single-spaced lines of writing vertically on a full sheet, the first line of writing will be on line (a) 26, (b) 28, or (c) 30.	____	9. ____
10. If a centered announcement contains 12 double-spaced lines, the number of lines required by the problem is (a) 12, (b) 23, or (c) 34.	____	10. ____
11. After a period following a personal initial, (a) space one time, (2) space two times, or (c) do not space.	____	11. ____
12. A hyphen is used to (a) join closely related words, (b) show separation of thought, or (c) show interruption of an idea.	____	12. ____
13. The proofreaders' mark that indicates "transpose" is (a) #, (b) ∽, or (c) ∧.	____	13. ____
14. The proofreaders' mark that indicates the removal of characters is (a) stet, (b) ⟋ᵟ, or (c) ⊏.	____	14. ____
15. Personal letters must contain (a) writer's keyed name, (b) letter address, or (c) salutation.	____	15. ____
16. When all letter parts are keyed flush with the left margin, the letter format is called (a) block, (b) standard, or (c) personal.	____	16. ____
17. If the writer's name is keyed below the complimentary close, return (a) two times, (b) three times, or (c) four times to key the name.	____	17. ____
18. On a small envelope, the letter address should be keyed (a) exactly centered, (b) slightly below and to the left of center, or (c) slightly above and to the right of center.	____	18. ____
19. The first item that should occur in a personal letter is the (a) date, (b) return address, or (c) neither the date nor return address.	____	19. ____
20. Words that must be divided at the end of a line should be divided only (a) between syllables, (b) if they contain more than six letters, or (c) four or more characters are carried to the next line.	____	20. ____

Formatting applications 2

for use after Lesson 31

a

Personal letter (LM p. 21)

1 Set margins for a 50-space line.
2 Format and key the letter. Divide words as needed, applying word-division guides (p. 73 textbook).
3 Proofread and correct all errors.
4 Address a small envelope.

words

2775 Demooney Road | College Park, GA 30349-2845 | November 13
12, 19-- | Ms. Joni Wattjes | 1105 South Park Drive | Miami, FL 27
33125-6821 | Dear Joni 31

As much as I enjoyed Atlanta, seeing you was a highlight of the AMA 45
workshop last week. Can you believe it has been five years since we 57
were in graduate school together? I can't! 68

Since I began working as a conference coordinator for AMA, I've had 81
an opportunity to travel and meet a lot of interesting people. The 95
"professional development" is certainly good for me, though I'm not 108
"rich and famous" as you predicted at IU--in fact, I'm neither. 121

I'm glad you're happy with your new job. Let's not wait until next 135
year's conference to talk over old times. Can you come here in the 149
spring, say, March 12, April 2, or April 30? 157

Sincerely | Tracy Montgomery 163

---

b

Paragraphs with title (plain sheet)

1 Set margins for a 60-space line.
2 Center the heading horizontally 11/2" from the top of the paper. Divide words as needed, applying word-division guides (p. 73 textbook).
3 Proofread and correct all errors.

THE DATABASE MANAGEMENT SYSTEM 6

A database management system will allow an office worker to 18
enter, store, and manipulate data. The data stored in a database 31
management system can be sorted and grouped to provide the 43
information needed for executive reports. 52

In the beginning, database products were just file managers. 64
Today they are used to generate complex reports for inventory 77
control, sales, accounting, maintenance, and other business areas. 90

Each group of information referring to a common subject is 102
called a record. For example, employee personnel information for 116
one person is entered as one record. A group of records is called a 130
file. The DBMS (database management system) allows the office 143
worker to sort the records in many ways. A list of employees who 157
work in a specific department or who have similar job positions could 169
be obtained from a database, for example. 177

Although the DBMS has many advantages, some companies 188
maintain that traditional filing systems are still needed for long-term 203
storage. A combination of the DBMS and paper storage offers a 215
workable alternative for many automated offices. 225

Basic skill: measurement

for use after Lesson 31

a
Straight copy

1 Set margins for a 60-space line.
2 Key two 1' writings on each ¶; determine *gwam*; proofread and circle any errors.
3 Key two 3' writings on both ¶s combined; determine *gwam*; proofread and circle any errors.

all letters used **E 1.2 si 5.1 awl 90% hfw**

	gwam 3'	
Because education is esteemed in the work world, your	4	36
drive to complete your course work may be quite strong. A	8	40
degree can help you earn a good management position. If you	12	44
work in a factory or in an office, a degree can help you excel	16	49
in your job.	17	50
The value of a good education is great. Not only is it	20	53
helpful in finding a job, it can also boost your zest for	24	57
life. An interest can branch out more than you ever thought	28	61
it could. A school can offer options not offered to you	32	65
elsewhere.	33	66

gwam 3' | 1 | 2 | 3 | 4 |

b
Statistical copy

1 Set margins for a 60-space line.
2 Key two 1' writings on each ¶; determine *gwam*; proofread and circle any errors.
3 Key two 3' writings on both ¶s combined; determine *gwam*; proofread and circle any errors.

all letters/figures used **E 1.2 si 5.1 awl 90% hfw**

	gwam 3'	
Will you order a book on travel (#478XZ) from the red	4	35
catalog on my desk. The book costs $25, or $20 when 4 or more	8	40
books are ordered at a time--this can save us 20%. I am sure	12	44
you will like the chapter "On the Road"; it is quite good!	16	48
Do write on the form the full name and order number of	20	51
each book we wish to order, and send an extra $1.25 with the	24	56
order--this is used to pay for shipping the books. A bill is	28	60
now subject to 6/10, net 30. Can't we order 4 books by 9/30?	32	64

gwam 3' | 1 | 2 | 3 | 4 |

Formatting applications 2, a, p. 19

Performance checkup A, a, p. 25

Performance checkup A

for use after Lesson 31

a
Personal letter (LM , p. 23)
1 Set a 50-space line.
2 Format and key the letter. If necessary, divide words at line endings according to word-division guides.
3 Proofread and correct all errors.

words

2212 South Park Lane | Cincinnati, OH 45227-4520 | February 2, 19-- 13
| Dear Dr. Voyles 16

(¶1) Remember me? I am one of your former students who used to get nervous 31
in front of your video camera. 37

(¶2) Believe it or not, I decided to become a business education teacher. At 52
last, I've concluded that I'll be happy teaching others the way that you once taught 69
me. Next fall I'll begin graduate classes at Ohio State University. Now you 84
know that the help you gave me at Georgia State was not all wasted! 98

Sincerely | Ms. Benita Moore 103

b
Invitation (plain sheet)
Center the invitation vertically DS; Center each line horizontally.

The Graduating Class of
TIFT COUNTY HIGH SCHOOL
announces the
Commencement Exercises
Friday, June 3, 1991
at 8 p.m.
Tift County Stadium

Performance checkup A (continued)

c

Paragraphs with title
(plain sheet)

1 Set a 60-space line.
2 Center the heading horizontally, 1 1/2" from the top of the paper. QS below the heading.
3 Format and key the report DS; divide words at line endings according to word-division guides.
4 Center the two items as shown.

CORPORATE ANNUAL REPORTS

Annual reports trace a corporation's past, depict its present, and provide useful information for anyone looking to its future. The purpose of an annual report is to allow its readers to make decisions on the basis of information it contains. Typical users include

stockholders and financial analysts

government agencies and the general public

Of these groups, stockholders are the main users of annual reports. Corporate management communicates "full and fair disclosure" to stockholders, who then use the information to provide direction for the company and, at the same time, to protect their own financial interests.

Communication skills workshop A

for use after Lesson 37

a
Apply capitalization rules
Format the ¶s with a 1 1/2" top margin and a 65-space line; provide capitalization as you key. If necessary, refer to page 78 (textbook).

it was a hot, steamy summer day in august. the crowd had gathered at eaton hall to hear their no. 1 candidate for state senate, sam waldren. since the fourth of july festivities had recently passed, the november election was on the minds of friends and family of incumbent senator waldren. the patriotic and conservative community was a mixture of both german and french descent.

after consuming a picnic dinner of hamburgers, hot dogs, baked beans, corn on the cob, german potato salad, and tossed salad with french dressing, the excited crowd gathered for the program. The master of ceremonies, dr. mason, attempted to quiet them by yelling, "let's begin down victory road to november." the response from the crowd was unanimous, "he's no. 1." dr. mason then directed the crowd to page 4 of their programs to sing the first and third verses of our national anthem.

b
Apply punctuation rules
70-space line; SS
Punctuate each sentence correctly as you key. Refer to page 79 (textbook) if necessary.

1 Nobuaki is very tan He likes his lifeguard job at the swimming pool
2 Dr. Michael Elmore's tenth anniversary with the corporation is May 19
3 The program began at 7 pm with Eva Valdez, DDS, being introduced
4 Dan explained to the workers, ". . . and management will support you"
5 Please stop at the office either before eight or after three tomorrow
6 The CEO of that corporation is a very famous and well-liked gentleman
7 What happened to my machine Was June using it for personal business
8 What time did she arrive Four Five Six Does anyone know exactly
9 Splendid It can't be true I don't believe it But it's twin boys
10 Prof Whitman begins in the fall The faculty favored her appointment
11 Impossible Something must be done about this by March 10 No later
12 The contract stated specifically, "There must be three . . . no more"
13 Payment is due early next week Please send it by Thursday afternoon
14 What organization did you join OEA FBLA DECA Are you an officer
15 I will do my best to have the information to IMB no later than July 1
16 May we have your answer soon Ms Winters, CPA, will be expecting it
17 There must be more materials In the warehouse In the shop Where
18 Who took this message What day did she call Was it before 10 am

Communication skills workshop A (continued)

c
Improve spelling and word usage skills

2" top margin; 70-space line SS; DS between 3-line groups

Key the "guide" sentences in each set *after* checking the corresponding guide words. Then key the "application" sentence, inserting the appropriate word in each blank as you key. (Do not underscore the inserted words). After you have keyed the 12 sentences, key the "application" sentences again, supplying the appropriate word for each blank.

Guide words

1. accept (receive; agree) . . . . except (omit; but)
2. access (entry; get at) . . . . excess (over limits)
3. advice (opinion) . . . . advise (give opinion)
4. affect (to influence) . . . . effect (result)
5. wait (stay) . . . . weight (make heavy)
6. weak (lacking strength) . . . . week (7 consecutive days)
7. wear (use for clothing) . . . . where (what place)
8. weather (state of atmosphere) . . . . whether (if; if not)

Guide 1 Everyone was there except Jessica, whose uncle would accept her award.
Guide 2 The excess load of the semitrailer prevented it access to the highway.
Application The broker will ______ your offer, which allows ______ to my property.

Guide 3 My boss will advise this move, but I must remember my friend's advice.
Guide 4 His wisdom will affect their lives, but the effect may never be known.
Application The ______ of the counselor's ______ will decide the college selected.

Guide 5 It is worth the wait to buy clothes that save weight in our suitcases.
Guide 6 Due to the weak cold front, it will be another week until cooler days.
Application Doug plans to ______ another ______ until the vice president is announced.

Guide 7 If I knew where the dinner will occur, I could select a dress to wear.
Guide 8 Tomorrow's weather will determine whether the sports are held outside.
Application My grandmother will decide ______ I ______ her silver bracelet tonight.

---

d
Proofread/revise as you key

70-space line DS

As you key each sentence, correct misspelled and misused words.

1 It has been aproximately a week since the comittee gave some advise.
2 Corprate headquarters gives access of personal skills to management.
3 The instalation of the satellite allows internattional whether status.
4 Please except this oportunity to receive the serveces of our faculty.
5 Monique does not know if the advice is apropriate for her situations.
6 It will be in Bob's best intrest to except the position in Personal.
7 The shipment was recieved yesterday accept it was imediately refused.
8 Employes of this company may find it neccesary to wait for insurance.
9 The custamers may accept the affect of these products on their health.
10 It is always good advise to wear light-colored clothes in hot whether.

Self-check questions 3
for use after Lesson 37

NAME ____________________

DATE ______________ SCORE __________

1 Write the letter for each correct answer in the blank at the right.
2 When you have answered all the items, check your answers below.

Answers	Text Page
1. a	78
2. a	78
3. b	79
4. c	79
5. c	81

Answers	Text Page
6. a	81
7. b	81
8. a	82
9. c	82
10. a	83

Answers	Text Page
11. b	83
12. b	83
13. a	83
14. b	83
15. b	85

Answers	Text Page
16. a	87
17. a	87
18. c	87
19. a	90
20. b	91

answers score

1. Do not capitalize (a) titles that follow a name, (b) nouns followed by identifying numbers, or (c) first words of direct quotations. . . . . . . ____ 1. ____

2. Capitalize (a) titles that precede personal names, (b) compass directions not part of a name, or (c) the word "page" if followed by a number. . . . . ____ 2. ____

3. Use a question mark after a direct question and follow it with (a) one blank space, (b) two blank spaces or (c) three blank spaces. . . . . . ____ 3. ____

4. An ellipsis is formed when ending a sentence by using (a) two, (b) three, or (c) four periods. . . . . ____ 4. ____

5. A personal/business letter must contain a (a) dateline, (b) return address, or (c) both a and b. . . . . ____ 5. ____

6. The margins for a short letter are set using a (a) 50-space line, (b) 60-space line, or (c) 70-space line. . . . . ____ 6. ____

7. The margins for an average letter are set using a (a) 50-space line, (b) 60-space line, or (c) 70-space line. . . . . ____ 7. ____

8. Below the complimentary close in a business or personal letter, strike the return key (a) four, (b) three, (c) two times before keying the sender's name. . . . . ____ 8. ____

9. Below the dateline in a letter, strike the return key (a) twice, (b) one, or (c) four times. . . . . ____ 9. ____

10. Special notations such as "PERSONAL" or "CONFIDENTIAL" on an envelope are placed a (a) DS below the return address, (b) DS below the stamp position, or (c) DS below the envelope address. . . ____ 10. ____

11. Mailing notations on an envelope, such as "SPECIAL DELIVERY" or "REGISTERED," are placed (a) on the second line of the mailing address, (b) a DS below the stamp position, or (c) a DS below the return address. . . . . ____ 11. ____

12. When inserting a letter in an envelope, place the last crease (a) toward top of the envelope, (b) toward the bottom of the envelope, or (c) facing the inside of the envelope. . . . . ____ 12. ____

13. When addressing large envelopes, the mailing address should be keyed (a) about 1/2 inch left of center, (b) about 3/4 inch left of center, or (c) about 3/4 inch right of center. . . . . ____ 13. ____

14. On a large envelope, the space between the top edge and the envelope address should be about (a) 1 1/2", (b) 2", or (c) 2 1/2". . . . ____ 14. ____

15. When preparing a letter on letterhead paper, do not key a (a) dateline, (b) return address, or (c) signature (sender's name) line. . . . . ____ 15. ____

16. A simplified interoffice memo does not contain a (a) return address, (b) dateline, or (c) reference initials. . . . . ____ 16. ____

17. The subject line of a simplified memo is keyed a DS below the (a) receiver's name, (b) sender's name, or (c) dateline. . . . . ____ 17. ____

18. Below the body of the simplified memo, (a) DS and key the reference initials, (b) DS and key the sender's name, or (c) QS and key the sender's name. . . . . ____ 18. ____

19. Block style means (a) all lines begin at the left margin, (b) all lines except the dateline begin at the left margin, or (c) all lines begin at the left margin but paragraphs are indented. . . . . ____ 19. ____

20. To compute *g-pram*, divide (a) total characters keyed by production time, (b) total words keyed by production time, or (c) total correctly keyed words by production time. . . . . ____ 20. ____

Formatting applications 3

for use after Lesson 37

a
Business letter (LM p. 31)

Format and key the business letter (average) on letterhead paper. Key the following return address immediately above the date:

750 Onyx Terrace, Suite A
Paterson, NJ 07508-1286

Address a large envelope; fold the letter for insertion. Refer to pages 85-86 (textbook) if necessary.

words

Current date | Mr. Steven Hernandez | P.O. Box 628 | Carrollton, GA 30117- 3
3296 | Dear Mr. Hernandez 18

(¶1) Here is the report you requested concerning the improvement of the Collec- 33
tions Department. 37

(¶2) The research conducted on the present system indicates two problems in the 52
Collections Department. First, an analysis of the letters we currently send shows 68
that our customers find them unclear. Second, procedures for delinquent ac- 83
counts are not being followed by the collection clerks. 95

(¶3) Two possible solutions which would improve our present collections rate are 110
detailed in the report. I believe you will agree that the more effective solution is 127
to establish a management position for this department. 139

(P4) If I can be of assistance in implementing either alternative, please let me know. 156

Sincerely | Mrs. Valorie Neal | Administrative Assistant | xx | Enclosure 168
envelope 180

---

b
Simplified memorandum
(plain sheet)

Format and key the simplified memo.

Current date | All Collections Clerks | COLLECTIONS MANAGER 12

(¶1) Ms. Chandra Wooldridge has joined our firm as Collections Manager. Her 26
responsibility will be to oversee the Collections Department and to maintain 41
efficient and effective operations. 49

(¶2) Ms. Wooldridge holds a B.B.A. degree in Administrative Systems and has 63
considerable experience in working with delinquent accounts. At her previous 79
place of employment, she designed a billing system which increased collections 95
by 17 percent in its first year of operation. 104

(¶3) Please welcome Ms. Wooldridge as a new member of our Collections Depart- 118
ment. I am sure you will enjoy working with her. 128

Steve Hernandez | xx 132

Communication skills workshop B

for use after Lesson 41

a

Apply plural formation rules

70-space line DS; 2" top margin

As you key each sentence, correct the misspelled plural forms. If necessary, check "Forming Plurals" on page 93 (textbook).

1 This restaurant has many specialtys, but his favorite is the lasagna.

2 City busses cause a great deal of air pollution with the gasses emitted.

3 Companys involved with the merger will meet the attorneys for dinner.

4 The children in Miss Wolf's science class learned to write hypothesis.

5 Go to the public librarys in the county to locate your three indexes.

6 Agendaes for the town board's meetings may be picked up today at three.

7 Television heroes were the topic of discussion in Chuck's drama class.

8 Music from two grand pianoes greeted the king's guestes in the ballroom.

9 While on my vacation in Hawaii, the two luaues were the most enjoyable.

10 Those warehouses stored hundredes of boxs from four different studioes.

11 Members from the local area churchs met at the high school gymnasium.

12 Contractores will make a bid on the bases of nine thousand square feet.

b

Apply rules for adding suffixes

70-space line DS; 2" top margin

As you key each sentence, correct the misspelled suffix forms. If necessary, check "Apply rules for adding suffixes" on page 94 (textbook).

1 The arriveal of Flight 2042 was late due to thunderstorms and flooding.

2 There's a better likelyhood of happyness if partners are in agrement.

3 Make sure you are separateing the egg yolk and egg white before mixing.

4 Because of all the argueing, they are forceing their views on coworkers.

5 Kenny was extremly courageous when he jumped into the freezing water.

6 Please be careful that your involvment does not create too much work.

7 The sight was not only awesome but extremly grusome for Mary to see.

8 Sara becomes quite exciteable when dining out in an elegant restaurant.

9 The children were moved to safty when the tornado signal was sounded.

10 Facilitys were made servicable for the handicapped after renovation.

11 Ordinaryly the heavyest cargo is worth more, but not in this instance.

12 Judgeing by the useage of water, the shortage of rain will be a problem.

13 We will go canoing this fall when the foliage turns brilliant colors.

14 Steve's new car makes driveing comforteable and relaxing for long trips.

15 Politness is a quality that many young people must evolve and retain.

Communication skills workshop B (continued)

c
Improve spelling and word usage skills

2" top margin; 70-space line SS; DS between 3-line groups

Key the "guide" sentences in each set *after* checking the corresponding guide words. Then key the "application" sentence, inserting the appropriate word in each blank as you key. (Do not underscore the inserted words). After you have keyed the 12 sentences, key the "application" sentences again, applying the appropriate word for each blank.

Guide words

1. aid (help) . . . . aide (assistant)
2. any one (one person; before "of") . . . . . . anyone (anybody)
3. aspect (phase) . . . . expect (anticipate)
4. assistance (help) . . . . assistants (helpers)
5. setting (environment) . . . . sitting (session)
6. some time (period of time) . . . . sometime (indefinite time)
7. steel (alloyed iron) . . . . still (motionless, quiet)
8. territory (geographical area) . . . . tertiary (third rank)

Guide 1 The nurses aide is trained to give aid to those who are storm victims.
Guide 2 If anyone is prepared for the test, I can excuse any one of you to go.
Application If ______ of the victims is seriously hurt, ______ must be administered.

Guide 3 Neil does not expect Stephen to know each aspect of reroofing a house.
Guide 4 Please get assistance from the foremen to ask one of their assistants.
Application Their ______ must know every ______ of the preparation procedures.

Guide 5 For our family's photo sitting, a summer outdoor setting was selected.
Guide 6 My dogs will arrive sometime soon but won't be released for some time.
Application It will be ______ until the crew begins ______ the props on stage.

Guide 7 The Gary steel mills become dark, still silhouettes along the horizon.
Guide 8 Our class explored the tertiary layer of rock in the rugged territory.
Application The vast ______ was engulfed by the ______ air and glowing moonrise.

---

d
Proofread/revise as you key

70-space line DS

As you key each sentence, correct misspelled and misused words.

1 Policies by the comission will be implementted some time in the future.
2 There's a possability reduced benifits will extend to the steal mills.
3 Maintanance and monitering are expects of the engineering departments.
4 Make sure the foreman is in complience of eligable return of material.
5 The ten permanent categorys for equipment are adaquate for some time.
6 The fire departments appreciate any aide given in capturing the animal.
7 During the photo setting, your assistants will be suffecient and kind.
8 Mr. Fierst does not expect a committment until all the facts are given.
9 Mrs. Hall was a teacher's aid during the testing of the junior class.
10 Anyone of us can be successful; it takes comittment and perseverance.

Formatting applications 4

for use after Lesson 41

Key the report at the right in unbound format DS.

Note: Indent enumerated items 5 spaces from the left margin.

Note: If your word processing program will not permit you to key superscripts, you may use the alternative format / # /.

words

ETHICS IN BUSINESS 4

The roots of American business ethics can be traced to the many immigrants 19
who came to this country and its "free enterprise" economy. Many of today's 34
corporations originated from family-owned businesses that grew by "doing the 50
right thing." Some, if not all, corporate philosophies still reflect the basic attitude 67
of doing what is right. 72

"Corporations should be concerned with corporate profits along with the 87
concept of human goods." [1] This statement reflects the author's belief that busi- 103
nesses are too concerned about the "bottom line" and too little concerned about 119
people. In fact, many articles have been written concerning a lack of social 135
responsibility, trading scandals, and unfair labor practices. Has something hap- 151
pened to American business ethics? 158

As a matter of fact, the examples of ethical business behavior are neither 173
new nor one sided. The Pecora investigation of 1933 was of even greater magnitude 189
than more recent "insider trading" scandals. An investigation set up by the U.S. 206
Senate to review the financial practices of lending institutions led to the Crash of 229
1929. Worthless securities were being unloaded to banking customers, and a 238
prominent financier of the era admitted to informing influential people of a new 254
issue of securities that could be sold to the "unwashed" public at a huge profit.[2] 271
None of the well-known people involved were charged for illegal practices because 287
they had not committed any crime. The Pecora investigation led ethical legislators 304
to pass the Securities Exchange Act of 1934. 313

A tragic drug tampering episode in the 1980s made the American public 327
aware of the need for high ethical standards in the corporate world. The drug 343
manufacturer's remarkable reaction and recovery from a crisis is an outstanding 359
example of strategic (bottom line) and ethical (humane) thinking. An evaluation 375
of the corporate philosophy could have predicted that the company would risk the 392
millions of dollars necessary to protect customers' lives.[3] 404

(continued on next page)

words

Societal changes have influenced business practices. Causes of increased 419
pressure for ethics in business include the following: 430

1. More women in the workforce. Demand for equal rights in the workplace 445
has enabled businesswomen to be successful in the corporate world. 458

2. Minorities on the move. Many top positions are being filled by minorities, 474
challenging many of the established traditions. 484

3. Older society. Concerns about seniority and retirement are on the rise 499
and are sure to increase as the average age of Americans goes up. 513

4. Tighter economy. Corporations are cutting back on costs by eliminating 528
many managerial positions. 534

Tough problems like ethics in business have not been solved in the decades 549
since immigrants began arriving on American shores; there are no quick fixes, 564
easy answers, or magic solutions. Ethics requires "eye-hand coordination"; only 580
by coordinating the eye for business with the hand for humanity can a company 596
develop a code of ethics that addresses its unique responsibility to American 612
society. 614

ENDNOTES 615

[1] T. Donaldson and T. Werhane, Ethical Issues in Business (New Jersey: 635
Prentice Hall, Inc., 1979), p. 86. 642

[2] P. Fuhrman, "The Securities Act of 1988," Forbes, January 9, 1989, pp. 658
40-41. 659

[3] A. Carroll, "Greater Concern for Ethics and the Bigger Back Yard," Man- 674
agement Review, February 1989, pp. 28-29. 685

REFERENCES 687

Carroll, A. "Greater Concern for Ethics and the Bigger Back Yard." Management 705
Review, February 1989. 711

Donaldson, T., and T. Werhane. Ethical Issues in Business. New Jersey: Prentice 733
Hall, Inc., 1979. 737

Fuhrman, P. "The Securities Act of 1988." Forbes, January 9, 1989. 752

Hanson, K. and R. Solomon. It's Good Business. New York: Antheneum Press, 771
1985. 772

Basic skill: measurement

for use after Lesson 41

a
Straight copy

1 Set margins for a 70-space line.
2 Key one 3' and one 5' writing; determine *gwam*.
3 Proofread and circle errors.

all letters used A 1.5 si 5.7 awl 80% hfw

gwam 3' | 5'

Everyone needs to use good manners, but a business executive may 4 3 53
find social graces essential when dealing with people from foreign 9 5 56
countries. Most schools do not teach etiquette, but many experts think 14 8 59
it should be offered. Fast foods and working parents have caused the 18 11 61
amount of time spent teaching good manners at home to be reduced. This 23 14 64
can be trouble for a business executive at home or abroad. 27 16 67

Good manners are the same for men and women in the United States, 31 19 69
but when traveling abroad some differences exist. In Japan, women in 36 22 72
business should always dress conservatively and should not eat alone in 41 25 75
public. The proper way for executives to greet in America is to shake 46 27 78
hands; but in South and Latin America, it is accepted among men and 50 30 80
women to air kiss on each cheek. Being on time may be important at 55 33 83
home, but a half hour delay is not unusual in many foreign countries. 59 36 86

We must remember that citizens of other countries are often baffled 64 38 89
by us as well. It is important to make our foreign acquaintances feel 69 41 92
at ease. This can best be done by putting forth an extra effort to 73 44 94
learn the customs of other countries and to be courteous at all times. 78 47 97
After all, good manners are simply a combination of common sense and 83 50 100
thinking of others. 84 51 101

gwam 3' | 1 | 2 | 3 | 4 | 5 |
5' | 1 | 2 | 3 |

b
Statistical copy

1 Set margins for a 70-space line.
2 Key two 3' writings; determine *gwam*.
3 Proofread and circle errors.

all letters/figured used E 1.2 si 5.1 awl 90% hfw

gwam 1' | 3'

Thank you for your request of the 29th. I am sorry we could not 13 4 40
reply to it before now, but the letter was mailed to 3478 Xenia--not 27 9 44
658 Zinnia Drive (which is now our local mailing address). We did not 41 13 49
get your letter until June 10. 47 16 51

We are pleased to reserve for you a single room (#794) for August 26 14 20 56
to 30. If you believe you might arrive after 4, won't you please forward 29 25 61
a 30% deposit of $58.50 to hold the room. We shall be happy to serve 42 30 65
you and hope you will enjoy your 5-day visit with us here at the Hotel 56 35 70
Washington. 58 36 71

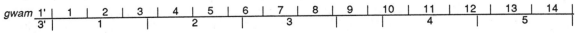

gwam 1' | 1 | 2 | 3 | 4 | 5 | 6 | 7 | 8 | 9 | 10 | 11 | 12 | 13 | 14 |
3' | 1 | 2 | 3 | 4 | 5 |

Self-check questions 4

for use after Lesson 47

NAME ____________________

DATE ______________ SCORE ______________

1 Write the letter for each correct answer in the blank at the right.

2 When you have answered all the items, check your answers below.

		answers	score
1.	To change a noun ending in *y* that is preceded by a vowel from singular form to plural, (a) add *s*, (b) change the *y* to *i* and add *s*, or (c) change the *y* to *i* and add *es*.	____	1. ____
2.	When adding a suffix beginning with a consonant to a root word ending in *e*, (a) drop the final *e*, (b) retain the final *e*, or (c) add an *e*.	____	2. ____
3.	Identify the incorrectly spelled word: (a) politely, (b) plentiful, or (c) managable.	____	3. ____
4.	The top margin for the first page of an unbound report is (a) 1 inch, (b) $1^1/_2$ inches, or (c) $2^1/_2$ inches.	____	4. ____
5.	The side and bottom margins for an unbound report should be about (a) $^1/_2$ inch, (b) 1 inch, or (c) $1^1/_2$ inches.	____	5. ____
6.	Most academic reports are (a) single-spaced, (b) double-spaced, or (c) as the student prefers.	____	6. ____
7.	On the first page of a report, the page number usually is (a) in the upper right-hand corner, (b) centered at the bottom margin, or (c) omitted.	____	7. ____
8.	Below the page number on a report, (a) double-space, (b) single-space, or (c) quadruple-space.	____	8. ____
9.	Long quotations (4 or more lines) within a report should be (a) single-spaced, (b) double-spaced, or (c) spaced the same as the copy in the report.	____	9. ____
10.	A reference listed within the body of a report is called a/an (a) end-note, (b) footnote, or (c) internal citation.	____	10. ____
11.	Supporting evidence is called (a) documentation, (b) reference, or (c) internal citation.	____	11. ____
12.	References (a) always begin on a separate page, (b) may begin on the last page of the body and continue onto the following page, or (c) may appear on the last page of the body if the references can be confined to that page.	____	12. ____
13.	The proofreaders' symbol to delete is (a) , (b)] [, (c)  . .	____	13. ____
14.	Select the sentence with correct number style: (a) I have seven ties and 11 shirts. (b) I have 7 ties and 11 shirts. (c) I have seven ties and eleven shirts.	____	14. ____
15.	Select the sentence with correct number style: (a) She inherited $4 million. (b) She inherited $4,000,000. (c) She inherited four million dollars.	____	15. ____
16.	Topic outlines are (a) single-spaced throughout, (b) double-spaced throughout, or (c) single-spaced with double-spacing above and below first-order topics.	____	16. ____
17.	For first-order topics in a topic outline, (a) all letters are capitals, (b) main words are capitalized, or (c) only the first word is capitalized. . .	____	17. ____
18.	The purpose of a resume is to (a) eliminate need for an application form, (b) obtain a job interview, or (c) follow up a job interview.	____	18. ____
19.	To place exactly half of a table to the right of center and half to the left of center, (a) backspace 1 space for every character in the longest line, (b) backspace 1 space for every 2 characters in the longest line, or (c) backspace 2 spaces for every character in the longest line.	____	19. ____
20.	To determine the top margin for vertical centering, subtract the total number of lines in the item from the total lines available and (a) begin keying on the next line, (b) subtract 1, or (c) divide by 2.	____	20. ____

Answers	Text Page
1. a	93
2. b	94
3. c	94
4. b	95
5. b	95
6. b	95
7. c	95
8. a	95
9. a	95
10. c	98
11. a	97
12. c	98
13. c	98
14. b	102
15. a	103
16. c	105
17. a	105
18. b	106
19. b	108
20. c	110

Communication skills workshop C

for use after Lesson 47

a
Apply number usage rules
70-space line DS; 2" top margin
As you key each sentence, change figures to words and words to figures as needed.

1 4 cheerleading squads picked 3 kinds of apples on September 18.
2 Their varsity squad has 3 seniors, two juniors, and 1 sophomore.
3 This year's Christmas mailing consists of over 500 customers.

4 When the bill is paid by the 10th, a two percent discount is available.
5 Ronald's next dentist appointment is the 16 of December at 4:15 p.m.
6 Used on the job last year were 1,000, 100 pound drums of crude.

7 Only 4 of the 10 bids submitted followed Specification Four, Page 12.
8 The 7th anniversary ceremony will begin promptly at 7 o'clock.
9 Your 3rd appointment for an estimate is at 2:30 p.m. on 5th Place.

10 Our contribution is $550--an increase of forty % from 1 year ago.
11 The coffee fund collects almost 50 dollars per week at only 20¢ per cup.
12 There are just 16 cars remaining--4 red, 3 white, four blue, & 5 black.

13 The cruise begins on the 12 through the 16 at a cost of $800 each.
14 85 percent of these bills are paid on the 10th of the month.
15 The address of the $2.1 million home is 1149 141 Avenue, Northwest.

b
Proofread/revise as you key
plain sheet, 1" side margins, begin on line 10
Format and key the simplified style memo at the right. Correct errors in number usage as you key; correct errors.

Current date | To All Building Products Customers | Insulation Shortage

(¶1) The critical shortage of 4 major chemical components for insulation was extensively discussed during the 11th Annual Building Products Meeting November 10th through 12. Sporadic production slowdowns at more than 100 plants has resulted in at least a fifty percent increase in labor costs.

(¶2) As a direct result of supply uncertainties, all insulation prices will increase more than 200 dollars per half a semitrailer shipment beginning the 1 of December.

(¶3) District 1 & District Nine will meet on December 4th at 10:30 a.m. at 1 Meridian Street, Chicago, Illinois, to discuss further implications of this shortage. Until additional information is available, provide for future price increases in all bids.

Neil J. Hall

xx

(continued on next page)

Communication skills workshop C (continued)

c

Improve spelling and word usage skills

2" top margin; 70-space line SS; DS between 3-line groups

Key the "guide" sentences in each set *after* checking the corresponding guide words. Then key the "application" sentence, inserting the appropriate word in each blank as you key. (Do not underscore the inserted words). After you have keyed the 12 sentences, key the "application" sentences again, supplying the appropriate word for each blank.

Guide words

1. cents (pennies) . . . . sense (meaning)
2. commence (to begin) . . . . comments (remarks)
3. cooperation (working together) . . . . corporation (business organization)
4. ensure (to make certain) . . . . insure (protect against loss)
5. expensive (costly) . . . . extensive (covering a large area)
6. fiscal (relating to finance) . . . . physical (relating to the body)
7. forth (away, forward) . . . . fourth (next after third)
8. perspective (view in correct proportion) . . . . . prospective (anticipated)

Guide 1 Common sense is invaluable in the managing of one's dollars and cents.
Guide 2 The convention will commence after comments are made by the president.
Application Mr. Bogg's opening ______ make good practical business ______ to all.

Guide 3 Sam's cooperation was appreciated by the president of the corporation.
Guide 4 Plan to insure your household belongings to ensure your peace of mind.
Application To ______ the success of the plan, everyone's ______ is required.

Guide 5 The extensive addition will undoubtedly be very expensive to maintain.
Guide 6 By fiscal year end, he must have a physical for his insurance carrier.
Application Achieving ______ fitness at a spa will be a very ______ endeavor.

Guide 7 This is the fourth time Brad has come forth with reliable information.
Guide 8 The prospective mother gained a new perspective after the appointment.
Application A broad ______ on policies was desired during the ______ quarter.

d

Proofread/revise as you key

70-space line DS

As you key each sentence, correct misspelled and misused words.

1 Pursuent to the decision authorized by Jim, we must insure his safety.

2 The fiscal plant facilitys will undergo extensive repairs tomorrow.

3 The chairman of the cooperation will recomend complete particepation.

4 This endustrial park will commense operations in the next fiscal year.

5 Referance to the forth page was made to the perspective shareholoders.

6 To acommodate the owners, arrangements were made to pay the morgage.

7 You will have full corporation when you use judgement and common cents.

8 The academic committee put fourth commence in their proper prospective.

9 Corespondence we previouslly received shows all the dollars and sense.

10 Ensure all extensive jewelry––especially the recently acquired pearls.

Formatting applications 5

for use after Lesson 47

Format and key tables and topic outline

4 plain sheets

a
Center the *(wide)* table horizontally and vertically.

words

GULFSOUTH CONFERENCE DIVISION II 7

			words
Jacksonville State	Jacksonville, AL	Bill Burgess	16
Mississippi College	Clinton, MS	John Williams	26
University of Tennessee	Martin, TN	Don McLeary	35
Valdosta State College	Valdosta, GA	Mike Cavan	44
West Georgia College	Carrollton, GA	Frank Vohun	54
Troy State	Troy, AL	Robert Maddox	61
Delta State	Cleveland, MS	Don Skelton	68
North Alabama	Florence, AL	Bobby Wallace	77
Livingston University	Livingston, AL	Sam McCorkle	87

b
Center the *(average)* table horizontally and vertically.

1990 WEST GEORGIA BRAVES 5

football schedule 9

			words
September 10	at Central Florida University	11 a.m.	19
September 16 7	at Jacksonville state	7 p.m.	26
October 1	at Livingston University	2 p.m.	35
October 15	Valdosta State	~~11 a.m.~~ 2 p.m.	49
October 8	Samford University	11 a.m.	42
October 22	at Mississipi ~~State~~ p College	5 p.m.	57
October 29	Delta State	3 2 p.m.	63
November 12	at Univ. (sp) of Tennessee	7 p.m.	72

c
Use a 2" top margin; center the *(narrow)* table horizontally.

EXPECTATIONS OF FIRST JOB 5

After College 8

Expectations	Percentage	words
Opportunities for promotion	73%	24
Job security	69%	27
Long-term income potential	65%	33
Benefits package	63%	37
Opportunities for creativity	61%	44
Above-average starting salary	53%	51
Favorable company location	50%	57

(Heading line "Expectations Percentage": 17 words)

(continued on next page)

Formatting applications 5 (continued)

d

Format an unbound report with table
(plain sheet)

Key the report DS. Center the *(narrow)* table horizontally.

Note: If you prepare a key line to center the table, do so on a separate sheet and set the required tab stops before beginning the report.

words

GOOD NEWS/BAD NEWS

4

Everyone writes letters, but does everyone compose correctly? Communi- 18
cation experts stress that there is a right way and a wrong way to 31
compose letters. For example, in "good news" letters, the main idea 45
should be included in the first paragraph, with supporting ideas 58
in the following paragraphs. "Bad news" letters are written with 71
a buffer in the first paragraph to soften the blow of the bad news. 85
The table shows some characteristics of both kinds of letters. 98

Good news	Bad news	Both	
Deductive	Inductive	"You attitude"	115
Good news first	Buffer first	Courteous tone	123

(Header row: 108)

Both types of letters incorporate the "you attitude" or 135
empathy for the reader. Letters have a stronger impact when the 148
material focuses on the reader. Try to avoid the use of I, we, 160
and our to achieve the "you attitude." Avoiding first-person 173
pronouns is especially important in bad news letters to indi- 185
cate that you are being fair and reasonable. This "you 196
approach" helps to maintain the goodwill of the receivers. 208

A positive close is also important in both types of letter. 220
In the closing paragraph you should show appreciation and, if 233
appropriate, indicate the action desired from the reader (action 246
ending). If you must be the bearer of an unfavorable mes- 257
sage, such as a refusal, try to offer an alternate solution, 269
ending on a positive note. A positive touch is much more 281
likely to achieve the desired action than a negative one. 292

Basic skill: measurement

for use after Lesson 47

a
Straight copy

1 Set margins for a 70-space line.
2 Key one 3' and one 5' writing; determine *gwam*.
3 Proofread and circle errors.

all letters used   A   1.5 si   5.7 awl   80% hfw

	gwam 3'	5'	
Each community has its own elected officials. States are divided	4	3	42
into districts from which officials are elected to operate the city and	9	6	44
county governments. To get the best person elected, all must vote.	14	8	47
Attention must be focused on a candidate's political history and what	18	11	50
he or she is willing to do for the people who will be served.	23	14	53
When studying a candidate's platform, you should take into account	27	16	55
his or her view on issues of concern. Decide what is important to you	32	19	58
and then decide if this candidate meets your needs. Even if you belong	37	22	60
to the same political party, you may not agree on major issues. It is	41	25	64
important that you study the platform of all candidates.	45	27	66
American citizens live in a society that affords them the privilege	50	30	69
and the obligation to vote for the officials to fill the offices of	54	33	71
local, state, and federal governments. The high-quality leadership that	59	36	74
built a great nation will cease to exist if you do not exercise your	64	38	77
right to vote!	65	39	78

gwam 3' | 1 | 2 | 3 | 4 | 5 |
5' | 1 | 2 | 3 |

b
Script copy

1 Set margins for a 70-space line.
2 Key two 3' writings; determine *gwam*.
3 Proofread and circle errors.

all letters used   A   1.5 si   5.7 awl   80% hfw

	gwam 3'	
Excitement is in the air in autumn. Fall brings with it many new	4	40
activities. You have old friends to see and new friends to make. Autumn	9	45
offers an opportunity to involve yourself with school and to emphasize	14	50
the extracurricular activities it has to offer.	17	53
Football season brings with it the opportunity to get involved in	22	57
many of the activities offered by your school. You can be a cheerleader,	27	62
join the drill squad, or be in the band. All of these activities support	32	67
your football team and intensify the spirit in your school.	36	71

(continued on next page)

Basic skill: measurement (continued)

for use after Lesson 47

c
Straight copy

1 Set margins for a 70-space line.
2 Key one 3' and one 5' writing; determine *gwam*.
3 Proofread and circle errors.

all letters used	A	1.5 si	5.7 awl	80% hfw

	gwam 3'	5'	
By the time you are an adult, you probably will have purchased a	4	3	40
car, leased an apartment, and acquired loans or credit cards. When you	9	6	43
borrow money to make these purchases, you are establishing a credit	14	8	46
history. These records are stored in a computer and many people have	18	11	49
access to this personal data.	20	12	50
It is relatively easy for anybody curious about your private life-	25	15	53
style to examine your computer record. You have the right by law to	29	18	55
know what data about you are maintained by anybody in any organization.	34	21	58
If any of your data are in error, you have the right to demand that	39	23	61
corrections be made.	40	24	62
Your right to privacy ensures that your personal data are given	45	27	65
only to individuals who have reason to see them. When someone sees your	49	30	67
personal data without just cause, that person is invading your privacy.	54	32	70
If you think that your privacy has been invaded for any reason, you	59	35	73
should explain your cause for concern to the local authorities.	63	38	76

gwam 3' | 1 | 2 | 3 | 4 | 5 |
5' | 1 | 2 | 3 |

d
Rough-draft copy

1 Set margins for a 70-space line.
2 Key two 3' writings; determine *gwam.*
3 Proofread and circle errors.

all letters used	A	1.5 si	5.7 awl	80% hfw

	gwam 3'	
To become successful in your career, you must posess a s	4	36
confidence in your ability to preform well on the job. People	8	40
who are confident attack business demands ~~problems~~ quickly. To gain	12	44
confidence in your job, you must learn to accept yourself for	16	48
who you are and who you can become. Once you realize that you	20	52
have many positive traits, express ~~accentuate~~ them. As your level of	24	56
confidence rises, you will find yourself eager ~~anxious~~ to tackle	28	60
any business problem which comes across your path to sucess.	32	64

Communication skills workshop D

for use after Lesson 47

a

Apply capitalization and number usage rules

Use a 60-space line DS; 1 1/2" top margin. Apply capitalization rules as you key and change figures to words and words to figures as needed.

References: pages 78, 102, and 103.

On tuesday, the 15 of november, the board of directors announced that the profit for the third quarter ending September 30th was up by almost 2.2%. Our president, dr. robert adams, expressed his gratitude for the dedication, support, and hard work from each employee-nearly 500.

The new Corporate Headquarters located at 1 Indiana plaza is scheduled for completion january 31st. Dedication ceremonies will be that afternoon beginning at two in the helen a. adams auditorium. A Reception will follow at the plaza hotel at four hundred fifty-four central plaza drive from 4 until nine o'clock. 11 employee committee representatives welcome your suggestions to make opening day Ceremonies a success.

---

b

Apply spelling and word usage rules

Use 1" side margins DS; 2" top margin. Supply missing punctuation and correct misspelled and misused words as you key.

References: pages 79, 80, 93, 94, and 104.

To insure corporation between IOSHA. and the industrial custumer, expensive safety orders must be posted immediately wear employes have excess to the information. Edward Reese, Ph.D, Labor Department, advices you of your responsibilities in his notice of Aug. 10 "... and the penalties listed are based upon extensive research."

After a forth violation of safety orders has been issued, it could be sometime before financial assistence can be rendered by the state. Each cooperation should comments its own reporting and use common cents... depending upon the judgement rendered by the authorized representative and the course of action previusly taken by management.

(continued on next page)

Communication skills workshop D (continued)

c
Improve spelling and word usage

2' top margin; 70-space line SS; DS between 3-line groups

Key the "guide" sentences in each set *after* checking the corresponding guide words. Then key the "application" sentence, inserting the appropriate word in each blank as you key. (Do not underscore the inserted words). After you have keyed the 12 sentences, key the "application" sentences again, supplying the appropriate word for each blank.

Guide words

1. feel (sense of touch) . . . . fill (raise the level of)
2. formally (in a formal manner) . . . . formerly (before)
3. hole (an opening) . . . . whole (entire)
4. lose (part with unintentionally) . . . . loose (not bound)
5. overdo (do too much) . . . . overdue (past due)
6. past (time gone by) . . . . passed (moved aong)
7. right (correct) . . . . write (to inscribe)
8. role (part in a play) . . . . roll (a list; type of bread)

Guide 1 Fill each container to the top so each student can feel the substance.
Guide 2 The formally attired crowd greeted the formerly renowned state leader.
Application Suzanne may ______ uneasy since most of the people are ______ dressed.

Guide 3 As each golfer approached the final hole, the whole gallery applauded.
Guide 4 Luis did not intend to lose the pages, but they were loose in his pad.
Application He will probably ______ the match since he did not birdie the last ______.

Guide 5 Because your exercise is long overdue, do not overdo your first class.
Guide 6 As the year passed, Randy knew his past performance would be rewarded.
Application Over a month has ______, and there is no news on the ______ accounts.

Guide 7 In order for each problem to be right, you must write every procedure.
Guide 8 Chi's name was pulled from the union roll to be cast in the lead role.
Application Make certain every name is spelled ______ on the teacher's master ______.

d
Proofread/revise as you key

Key the memo at the right in simplified format. Correct all errors as you key. Use the information below.

Date: **November 17, 19--**
Recipient: **Support Staff**
Subject: **Employee Relations**
Sender: **Devore Daniels**

		words
	words in heading	10
Each year employes of our support staffs are invited to attend		22
a (2)-day conference. To acommodate app personnell, we must know		35
by december 5 if you will be able to attend. The categorys		47
covered during these sessions arein complience with the univer-		60
sity evening school program. The schools commission will give		73
acadimic assistance to those eligable at the end of this confer-		87
ence. ¶ Monitoring of benefits, committee participation, customer		98
services, and corporate/international relations are just a few of the		112
topics referenced. We want you to fill that your participation		125
and comments are ~~enthusiastically~~ welcome--thy are. This con-		135
ference will effect your roll in your day-to-day work activities.		147
xx		147
	words in closing	150

Basic skill: measurement

for use after Lesson 50

a
Straight copy

1 Set margins for a 70-space line.
2 Key one 3' and one 5' writing; determine *gwam.*
3 Proofread and circle errors.

all letters used | A | 1.5 si | 5.7 awl | 80% hfw

	gwam 3'		5'
Stress is quite evident in every aspect of life. Stress is described	5	3	53
as anything that can cause physical or mental tension. It is not always	9	6	56
a result of something unpleasant, such as a test. Getting married or	14	8	59
going on a vacation, generally happy occasions, may cause mental pressure.	19	11	62
The purpose of stress management is not to free people from stress but	24	14	65
to keep it under control--to use it to reach goals.	27	16	67
To deal with stress, you must deal with the cause of it. If stress	32	19	69
comes from assignments not finished on time, prioritize them to reduce	37	22	72
anxiety. Practice flexibility and accept things not quite perfect.	41	24	75
Sometimes holding a firm position can cause you more stress than being	46	28	78
flexible. Everyone must learn to compromise at some time or another.	50	30	80
Also, no one is perfect; so do not expect yourself or others to be.	55	33	83
Once you have formed a stress management plan, just use it; and	60	36	86
your chances to be contented with life will increase considerably. Your	65	39	89
environment can be seen in a better light when you do not feel pressured	70	42	92
to achieve more than you can manage. You can also deal with relation-	74	44	95
ships on a more positive basis. You will find that good business and per-	79	47	98
sonal relationships can easily be developed when stress is not a factor.	84	50	101

gwam 3' | 1 | 2 | 3 | 4 | 5
5' | 1 | 2 | 3

b
Script copy

1 Set margins for a 70-space line.
2 Key two 3' writings; determine *gwam.*
3 Proofread and circle errors.

all letters used | A | 1.5 si | 5.7 awl | 80% hfw

	gwam 3'	
Proper preparation before a job interview is the key to obtaining	5	41
the right job. It is important that you should examine, analyze, and	9	45
evaluate the company, while at the same time determining what you have	14	50
to offer it. This information should be summed up in a letter.	18	54
The letter of application should establish quickly how you learned	23	59
about the job, what past experiences relate to the job, and how the	27	63
employer can call you for an interview. A letter that is error-free and	32	68
written clearly helps to create a positive first impression.	36	72

Performance checkup B

for use after Lesson 50

a
PC1 Table (plain sheet)
Use a 2" top margin; center the *(narrow)* table horizontally.

			words
STATES OF AUSTRALIA			4
By Population in Mid-Eighties			10
State	Square Kilometer	Population	23
New South Wales	801,428	5,401,881	30
Victoria	227,600	4,019,478	35
Queensland	1,727,000	2,587,315	41
Western Australia	2,525,500	1,440,607	49
South Australia	984,377	1,345,945	56
Tasmania	68,331	436,945	60

b
PC2 Simplified memo
(LM p. 49)
Format and key the simplified memo.

October 13, 19-- | Janet Silverstein, Personnel Manager | APPLICANTS FOR LEAD 15
WORD PROCESSING OPERATOR 20

All the applicants sent to me from your department have been interviewed. I am 36
now ready to make a recommendation for the position of lead word processing 51
operator. 53

Although Jim Lyman seems to be extremely knowledgeable in word processing 68
and is an excellent keyboard operator, I believe he may have some difficulty in 84
getting along with others and accepting a position of authority. Lauren Phoenix 100
has a college degree in Administrative Systems and also has a good background 116
in word processing. She has excellent human relation skills. Although Lauren 132
was employed just five months ago, she is willing to work overtime to increase her 148
knowledge of the company's procedures and the personnel who originate docu- 163
ments. 164

Jim and Lauren are the most qualified applicants for this position, but because 181
of Lauren's educational background and her ability to work well with others, I 197
am recommending her for the position of lead word processing operator. 211

Willa Mae Johnson, Information Systems Manager | xx 220

c
PC3 Table (plain sheet)
Center the *(average)* table vertically and horizontally.

BIRTHDATES OF FAMOUS AMERICANS			6
Since 1900			8
Name	Profession	Birthdate	18
Louis Armstrong	Musician	1900	24
Neil Armstrong	Astronaut	1930	30
Leonard Bernstein	Composer	1918	36
John F. Kennedy	President	1917	42
Billie Jean King	Tennis player	1943	50
Martin Luther King, Jr.	Minister	1929	57
Sandra Day O'Connor	Supreme Court Justice	1930	66

Apricot Crafts

750 Onyx Terrace, Suite A
Paterson, NJ 07508-1286
(201)663-0845

LM p. S1. LM page references in the textbook refer to Division 1 Laboratory Materials.

33c, Problem 1, page 84

Real Estate
Enterprises, Inc.

RE
EI

962 Earls Court Road
Salt Lake City, UT 84119-2037

Real Estate
Enterprises, Inc.

REEI

962 Earls Court Road
Salt Lake City, UT 84119-2037

Sedgwick Place Retirement Community

2767 Morning Star Drive
Phoenix, AR 85023-3130

Supplementary communication activity, page 104 (2)

<u>*Sedgwick Place Retirement Community*</u>

2767 Morning Star Drive
Phoenix, AR 85023-3130
(602) 731-5889

Stone
Public Relations and Marketing Agency
302 University Avenue Suite 2036 Seattle, WA 98101-0231

Stone Public Relations and Marketing Agency

302 University Avenue Suite 2036 Seattle, WA 98101-0231 (206) 555-3460

Stone
Public Relations and Marketing Agency
302 University Avenue   Suite 2036   Seattle, WA   98101-0231

Stone Public Relations and Marketing Agency
302 University Avenue Suite 2036 Seattle, WA 98101-0231 (206) 555-3460

Stone
Public Relations and Marketing Agency
302 University Avenue Suite 2036 Seattle, WA 98101-0231

Stone Public Relations and Marketing Agency

302 University Avenue Suite 2036 Seattle, WA 98101-0231 (206) 555-3460

Real Estate Enterprises, Inc.
RE EI
962 Earls Court Road
Salt Lake City, UT 84119-2037

Real Estate
Enterprises, Inc.

RE
EI

962 Earls Court Road
Salt Lake City, UT 84119-2037